DESIGN FOR LEA

USER EXPERIENCE IN ONLINE TEACHING AND LEARNING

Jenae Cohn
Michael Greer

NEW YORK   2023

"*Design for Learning* is a compelling read that not only demystifies teaching and learning practices, but also reimagines the way we think about the connective power of digital learning spaces in our changed world. I found myself nodding, grinning, and cheering as I poured through the chapters, as Cohn and Greer's personalities sparkled within the prose, bringing their humanity and heart to our broad work in education."

—Angela Gunder,
Chief Academic Officer, Online Learning Consortium

Good learning experiences combine content and context, and *Design for Learning* masterfully navigates readers through the journey of making better learning experiences. The authors provide context with just enough theoretical backing to provide a solid foundation for action, regardless of the reader's background in the topic.

—Cara North,
Owner of The Learning Camel, an Instructional Design Agency

Jenae Cohn and Michael Greer have woven together expert argument and insight in this wonderful book about how to design for learners and learning. Using rich examples and relatable explanations, they surface the various ways that learning happens beyond a classroom while connecting the dots between a learning designer's intentions and the actual learning experience. If you design or facilitate digital learning experiences of any kind, then you need to read this book.

—Lorna Gonzalez,
Director of Digital Learning at California State University
Channel Islands

This is a thorough and thoughtful guide for designing good learning experiences. Jenae and Michael have so much practical and concrete experience that they share in this book.

I particularly appreciated how thoughtful the authors were about considering the experience from the learner's point of view and the emphasis they put on learner agency. Increasingly, learning experiences are going to be online, so having a good guide for creating digital resources is very important for learning design.

—Julie Dirksen,
Author, *Design for How People Learn*

Cohn and Greer offer a practical set of processes and heuristics for designing interactive online learning environments that place the student at the heart of the design experience. Throughout the text, you'll find specific tables and activities to jump-start your design process, as well as examples of effective online assignments, with concrete takeaways at the end of each chapter. If your goal is to create engaging, human-centered online learning experiences, this is a book you will return to over and over!

—Mary Stewart,
Associate Professor of Literature and Writing Studies,
CSU San Marcos

Design for Learning
User Experience in Online Teaching and Learning
By Jenae Cohn and Michael Greer

Rosenfeld Media, LLC
125 Maiden Lane
New York, New York 10038
USA

On the Web: www.rosenfeldmedia.com
Please send errata to: errata@rosenfeldmedia.com

Publisher: Louis Rosenfeld
Managing Editor: Marta Justak
Interior Layout: Danielle Foster
Cover Design: Heads of State
Illustrator: Danielle Foster
Indexer: Marilyn Augst
Proofreader: Sue Boshers

ISBN: 1-959029-16-9
ISBN 13: 978-1-959029-16-8
LCCN: 2023938228

Printed and bound in the United States of America

HOW TO USE THIS BOOK

Who Should Read This Book?

Design for Learning is a resource for anyone who wants to design a course, training, or webinar that's interesting, engaging, and informative. We know that a lot of online courses can be disappointing. This book will give you the tips that you need to make yours really stand out.

Whether you're designing a formal course or a one-off workshop, you'll face huge opportunities and big challenges. We'll provide both theory and practical guidance so that you can meet these opportunities and challenges head-on, no matter whether you're an instructional designer, learning and development professional, instructional technologist, multimedia developer, UX specialist, content creator, or a teacher. We recognize that many of these roles overlap, so if you're designing a learning experience, you may be creating the lesson plans, designing the multimedia, and delivering the course material all at once. This advice will help you if you're supported by a team, or if you're designing an entire learning experience by yourself.

What's in This Book?

We move sequentially through the learning design process in this book, starting from the course ideation and planning stage all the way to the actual facilitation of the learning experience, ending with tips on how readers can evaluate and research the efficacy of the online course they've developed.

Chapter 1 sets the context, exploring why UX principles and practices are essential to understanding and designing a learning experience that's really going to work. The chapter ends with a learning design framework that will guide readers through the course development process that follows in the subsequent chapters.

Chapter 2 describes the first step in the learning design process: researching who the learners are going to be in the class you're building. Suggestions for conducting basic user research are provided along with some sample exercises that learning designers can conduct in order to start their course development process with their end users in mind.

Chapter 3 provides strategies for articulating clear course outcomes and building a course map that will help designers understand, at a high level, where their course will start and end. This chapter urges readers to think backward and consider where they want learners to wind up by the time the course is completed.

Chapter 4 explains what makes an online learning space so distinct from an on-site experience and provides examples of what factors a designer should consider in order to make sure that the learning experience is specifically designed for an online environment, rather than attempting to retrofit an on-site experience into an online space.

Chapters 5, 6, and 7 take a deeper dive into building the assets for an online course experience. Chapter 5 focuses specifically on what it means to design and produce text, specifically engaging with UX writing strategies for course development contexts. Chapters 6 and 7 detail what it takes to plan and produce instructional videos, considering how different kinds of instructional videos may be necessary for different parts of the course experience. All three chapters consider when and how different media may be most appropriate for the goals and outcomes a designer has developed within a course.

Chapters 8 and 9 focus on course facilitation and what it looks like to actually run a course once learners are actively participating in it. Chapter 8 provides tips for live, webinar experiences specifically while Chapter 9 focuses on strategies for engaging learners, whether they're participating in the class in real time or whether they're taking the course at their own pace. These chapters consider how all learners can feel like they belong in the experience and how facilitators can build inclusion into the design.

Chapters 10 and 11 invite designers to take a step back and consider strategies for assessing how successful learners have been in the course. Chapter 10 offers strategies for designers to test students' understanding of the course material, helping designers think through multiple strategies for seeing whether learners have, in fact, been learning throughout the course. Chapter 11, on the other hand, invites designers to assess the efficacy of their design, considering what research or information they may gather to determine whether the structure, pacing, activities, and assets designed for the course helped or hindered learning.

By the end of the book, designers should have a clear understanding of what it takes to build a course from start to finish and should be able to recognize what revision for a course might look like in the future.

What Comes with This Book?

This book's companion website (rosenfeldmedia.com/books/design-for-learning) contains a blog and additional content. The book's diagrams and other illustrations are available under a Creative Commons license (when possible) for you to download and include in your own presentations. You can find these on Flickr at www.flickr.com/photos/rosenfeldmedia/sets/.

FREQUENTLY ASKED QUESTIONS

Why are you applying user experience (UX) frameworks to designing and teaching trainings and courses?

We noticed that UX researchers and practitioners deal with challenges similar to those that online learning designers and facilitators face: organizing complex content collections; creating meaningful pathways through information; making ideas and information accessible; designing for platforms and screens of different sizes and affordances; responding to the needs of users with diverse skills and comfort levels with technology; and making online information usable.

Given these overlapping challenges, we came to the conclusion that UX theories, frameworks, and ideas could help online instructors and learning designers make good strategic decisions about course design, organization, and pedagogy. Specifically, ideas from UX can help to build understanding and empathy with learners, which we're confident will lead to better outcomes for everyone. To take a deeper dive into understanding the important points of intersection between UX practice and learning design, see Chapter 1.

I've been asked to design a course in just a month. Will this book help me design a course that quickly?

We understand that a lot of designers often have pretty tight turnarounds! While we would recommend having more time to develop a course using the principles suggested in this book, we have created advice that could be applied on shorter or longer timelines. Specifically, we call out how you could modify some of the design approaches for shorter (or longer) amounts of time in Chapters 2 and 3. In the chapters about video planning and production (Chapters 6 and 7), we also incorporate tips to make simpler videos in case you don't have time to engage in an extensive video planning and editing process.

How do I design a course that really keeps people's attention online?

When it comes to online learning, distraction is one of the biggest concerns, and we know that engagement metrics are a huge part of how designers can tell if a course is really engaging. We make the case that the more a course is targeted to whom *your* specific learners are and what their needs or concerns might be, the better you'll be able to serve them. (See Chapter 2 to understand where your learners might be coming from.) We also have a lot of specific strategies for keeping learners' attention once the course is running (see Chapters 8 and 9).

Is it really possible to create an online course or training that's just as good as an on-site one?

We think so! But it's important for readers of this book to recognize that an online learning experience is going to be really different than an on-site one. Comparing the two experiences is (forgive the cliché), a lot like comparing apples and oranges. You have to have different expectations up front—and so do your learners. In Chapter 4, we explore what unique advantages and limitations there are around building a course in an online space and consider how the lessons from UX research can inform quality experiences online. Chapters 8 and 9 are also good places to consult if you want to see a range of activities and interactions online that we think can uniquely spur connections between and among learners in a class community.

How will I know if the online course I'm designing is of high quality?

Measuring quality can be subjective; what's a good experience for one person may not be a good experience for someone else. That said, providing clear expectations, consistency, and structure to a course will, generally speaking, lead to positive experiences. See Chapter 3 for some examples of what it looks like to create enough structure within a course to ensure that it's clear to learners what they can expect from the course experience. If you're looking more for information about what it means to assess the impact of the course you've designed and demonstrate its good quality, see Chapter 11 for strategies and basic approaches to receiving feedback from learners on their course experience.

CONTENTS

FOREWORD

In 2006, just out of grad school, I was hired to teach and work at a community college in Massachusetts. The course: *FYE 101, First Year Experience*. My new boss handed me a copy of the previous professor's syllabus and the textbook. The latter was dense, expensive, and to be honest, pretty boring. It never occurred to me to force something onto my students that I was unwilling to bear myself, so instead, I asked my boss if I could redesign the course, completely, from the ground up.

"As long as you teach to the course objectives, you can do anything you want," he said.

That I did. I began with those course objectives, along with what I knew about my incoming students (a group of about 30 recent high-school graduates who were conditionally accepted at the local four-year institution, as long as they could first succeed at our community college), my own good and bad experiences as a learner, library books on pedagogy and design, and a lot of internet research. Over the next several months, I designed a course that went on to win me a teaching award and was eventually expanded as a requirement for most of our college's first-time students.

It sounds a bit romantic, doesn't it? Nostalgia and all. It was anything but.

Since I was a full-time staff person teaching as an adjunct, most of the designing happened outside of my work hours, on nights and weekends. I remember being surrounded by piles of papers and lesson plans while sitting at the dining room table I'd inherited from my late grandmother. I sat at that table, day in and day out, for three months. I had no idea what I was doing, which can be exhilarating and great for creativity, but also I had *no idea what I was doing*. Whenever I'd mention that I was redesigning the course from scratch to the other educators I'd encounter at my new workplace, they'd look at me like I had ten heads. The course ended up being weird, messy, and fun. By and large, it worked.

A year later, because of this initial success, the dean asked me to create an online section of the course, so I went through the design process all over again. Requesting piles of books about online teaching from the library, working outside of work hours, scouring the internet endlessly for ideas that would engage my new online learners. I quickly learned that online teaching is not the same as on-site teaching. I had to unlearn and relearn what it meant to engage my students. After getting my on-site course off the ground, I was back to square one. And with each term that I taught my online course, I felt like I was always taking one step forward and two steps back. After a few years of constantly revamping the course, I said to myself, "This is it. I'm exhausted and stressed. The course is fine. I'm not changing anything this term. I need to get a life."

Lies. Like many of you, I can't sit on my hands if there's something I can do to improve the learning experience for my students. And my "throw-spaghetti-at-the-wall" design model was wearing on me, really wearing on me. I'm confident in saying that my nearly 44-year-old self could not, would not, suffer through what my 20-something self did in the name of engaging design. Through a combination of naivete, anxiety, and my internal ADHD motor, I designed these early courses for myself and my learners. But I have often looked back at those times in my career and wondered if there was a better way. Back then, perhaps not. Now, absolutely.

Design for Learning: User Experience in Online Teaching and Learning brings together the best information we have about what goes into a quality online learning experience for this moment in higher education's history. For these students, the ones we have right now. For these faculty, the ones we have right now. It is a tool I wish I could gift to my younger self.

You will learn, for example, how to create a foundation for your course design that sets you up for success, investing time in the critical beginning stages of the design process that will save you time in the future. You'll learn how content development and facilitation are two sides of the same coin,[1] and how to consider both in your design process. You'll learn, in this one book, everything that I was

---

1 Gratitude to my friend, Michelle Pacansky-Brock, who introduced this "two sides of the same coin" concept to me. Michelle shared with me that she first heard it from Lené Whitley-Putz. You can read more here: https://onlinenetworkofeducators.org/2018/01/30/two-sides-coin/

scrambling and juggling to find in about a thousand different places for so many years. It's all in here, and in our era of overwhelm, I have immense respect for the folks who can gather and curate information for us, putting it all in one place for our weary, teaching souls.

For many of us who consider ourselves learning experience designers, the cornerstone of our work is and always has been empathy. As we face daily news of student and faculty disengagement, a mental health and burnout crisis, and attacks on diversity, equity, and inclusion, it can feel impossible to get our bearings.

As adrienne maree brown writes, "The crisis is everywhere, massive massive massive. And we are small." But, and this is a *big* but, brown also reminds us that if change is inevitable (and it is), then every pebble tossed in the river, every small action, can create massive shifts downstream. In fact, brown also writes, "Small is all."[2] Learning how to design a quality, online course from a foundation of empathy might feel like a small thing. I can promise you that it's not.

Wherever you are in your design and pedagogy journey, wherever you educate learners in the higher ed ecosystem, wherever you sit in this era of crisis, there are tools here to guide you toward creating learning experiences that work for you and your students. I don't know how or even if we will emerge from this era, but I do know, at some point, we're going to have to try, to at least try, to design a better world, a more humane world, for all life on this planet. We will all be students. We will all be teachers. And we will all benefit from simple, clear, practical guidance, like that found in *Design for Learning,* to help us gather and share both old and new lessons with each other.

—Karen Costa,
faculty development facilitator, adjunct faculty, and author

---

2   www.akpress.org/emergentstrategy.html

INTRODUCTION

Online Partners, Zoom, and Soup!

Believe it or not—we, Jenae and Michael, wrote this book without ever having met each other once in person! It always shocks people when we tell them that. Actually, we first met online by volunteering at the same professional organization, the Global Society of Online Literacy Educators, which is committed to sharing and creating resources specifically about *teaching writing online*.

Then we followed each other on social media, and one day, Michael saw a tweet that Jenae posted about book history. He reached out via email and insisted on connecting through Zoom. Many Zoom calls later, we discovered that we shared common interests beyond teaching writing courses: for example, geeking out over learning design, complaining about bad educational technology, creating websites, buying beautiful books, and cooking elaborate soups.

So even though Michael lives in Colorado, Jenae lives in California, and neither of us has ever worked at the same place, we found that our ideas kept orbiting on the same wavelength. We thought about writing blog posts together, but as we kept drafting those, we reconsidered and thought, why not write a book? Every one of our posts had a coherent conceptual arc, and it struck us that there was more we could do with continuous prose than discrete posts. Plus, Jenae had just finished writing her first solo book, and Michael was the only person who read and commented on all 300 pages of it. (Kudos to Michael!)

Long story short, we reached out to Rosenfeld Media and submitted a proposal—because the book bug had bitten both of us.

As online learning enthusiasts, writing together from a distance demonstrated a proof of concept that's at the very heart of this book: learning with someone else online takes care, intention, and open-mindedness. But we did it. If nothing else, the joint writing really proved to us that you *can* build meaningful relationships at a distance.

One thing we knew for sure: We had to combat the negative feelings and associations that most people have about online learning. We'd heard all of the complaints: "Learning online isn't 'real,'" "You can't get to know anyone online," and "Learning online is not as effective as learning in person." We've both been frustrated by these complaints and concerns, often ones which were shared with not a lot of evidence-based experience. We believe, however, that this book will dispel those beliefs for you *and* your students.

Oh, and if you're looking for some soup ideas, we've got you covered there as well.

MICHAEL'S SPICY BUTTERNUT SQUASH SOUP

We love to visit Santa Fe in the fall. This spicy soup brings back memories of trips to northern New Mexico, where the flavors and sunlight are always strong.

Adjust the amount of chile powder you use depending on your taste. The spice will grow on you with each bite, and you can use sour cream to tame things down if needed.

Ingredients

1 large butternut squash	2 tablespoons chile powder
2 tablespoons olive oil	4 cups chicken broth
1 small red onion, diced	Sour cream, for garnish
3 cloves garlic, roasted	Fresh cilantro, chopped, for garnish
6 plum tomatoes, diced	Preheat oven to 350 degrees

1. Using a sharp knife, punch several holes in the squash so it vents. Microwave the squash for 5 minutes (this helps to soften it up so it's easier to slice). Slice the squash lengthwise, scoop out any seeds, and place the squash cut side down in a baking dish and add about an inch of water. Bake for an hour or until it is very soft. Let the squash cool and then scoop out the flesh.

2. Using a large soup pan, heat the olive oil on medium until it's hot. Add the onions and sauté for 3 to 4 minutes. Add the roasted garlic and stir for another minute or two.

3. Add the tomatoes and simmer for 5 minutes. Add the chile powder and cook for 1 to 2 minutes, stirring often so the chile powder doesn't scorch.

4. Stir in the squash and chicken broth and simmer on low heat for 30 minutes.

5. If you have an immersion blender, use it to puree the soup until it is smooth. Or pour the soup into a blender and puree until smooth.

6. Reheat the soup and season with salt and pepper. Garnish with sour cream and cilantro. We like to stir the sour cream in at the end and swirl it around to make patterns in the orange soup.

Adapted from Joan Stromquist, *Santa Fe Hot and Spicy*. Santa Fe: Tierra Publications, 1998.

JENAE'S MISO MATZO BALL SOUP

Coming from a Jewish family, matzo ball soup is a favorite Passover holiday tradition. I wanted to mix it up and make something a little different this past year and noticed that a lot of flavors from Japanese cuisines overlap with those of traditionally Jewish and Eastern European foods. I looked up a variety of matzo ball soup and miso soup recipes and basically mashed them together the best that I could. This soup packs a pretty solid umami punch!

Ingredients

For the matzo balls:

2 large eggs

1 tablespoon canola oil

½ cup matzo meal

1 teaspoon baking powder

½ teaspoon salt

¼ teaspoon pepper

1 teaspoon furikake seasoning (or scallions)

For the soup:

1 quart miso-based broth (either prepackaged or could be made by blending miso paste in water)

1 teaspoon rice vinegar

1 tablespoon sesame oil

5–10 oz shiitake mushrooms (just depending on how "mushroomy" you like your soup to be)

2–3 large carrots

2–3 celery stalks

Seaweed (to your taste)

1. *Prepare the matzo balls.* In a small bowl, whisk together the eggs and canola oil. Add the matzo meal, baking powder, salt and pepper and any other seasonings you choose to include. Mix to combine fully. I recommend furikake to give this fusion dish an extra kick, but you could use scallions or green onions instead. Once combined, let the mixture sit in the refrigerator for 20–30 minutes.

2. *Prepare the soup.* In a Dutch oven or standard stock pot, heat up your broth. If you've purchased prepared broth, bring it to a gentle simmer. If you want to make your miso stock from scratch, pour roughly 4 cups of water in, bring it to a simmer, and then scoop in as much miso paste as you'd like (generally, I'd use 2–3 tablespoons of white miso paste, though red miso paste can work just as well; white miso paste tends to be milder than red miso paste). Add in your seaweed if desired.

3. *Add the vegetables into your soup.* Once the broth (and optional seaweed) has been brought to a gentle simmer, add mushrooms, celery, and carrots to the pot. Cover the pot and let the vegetables cook until *partially* soft, just 3–5 minutes. Do not cook them all the way since you'll be cooking the vegetables with the matzo balls in just a moment.

4. *Cook matzo balls in the soup.* Remove your matzo ball mixture from the refrigerator. Get your hands wet, and then roll the matzo ball mixture into roughly tablespoon-size balls. Carefully, add the matzo balls into the soup. Gently simmer with the matzo balls in the soup uncovered until the matzo balls are fluffy and buoyant. This should take about 15 minutes.

5. *Add additional seasoning.* Once all of the vegetables and matzo balls have cooked, add rice vinegar and sesame oil to the broth. Stir to combine and taste to your liking. Top with additional scallions, seaweed, or furikake seasoning!

Learning Is an Experience

A group of fifteen people log on to a video conference call together. They are gathered to attend a change management training session, all logging in from different locations. Their faces float in their individual squares, arranged in a neat grid. One minute before the session begins, the grid of faces shifts to the side of the screen and is displaced by a screen-shared "welcome" slide. The facilitator for the session announces that the conversation will begin shortly.

But what's called a "conversation" is not really a conversation. The facilitator talks for an hour as she progresses through a slideshow. The participants in their separate squares simply listen. Maybe some of them take notes. Others tune out.

Live online learning experiences like this are common, but they can often feel uninspired and, frankly, boring.

You could probably make your own list of online learning experiences gone wrong. The slide deck with tiny type that was almost unreadable. The endless blocks of dense informational text that had to be navigated in a pop-up window that looked like it was designed in the 1990s. A "next" button that can only be double-clicked for some reason. A workshop lacking clear organization and degenerating into chaos. Videos that lack captions. Seminars running over time—by an hour or more. The examples go on and on. But learning designers can do better than all of this.

Doing better means understanding that learning experiences can't just be *facilitated*; they must be *designed* in ways that are attentive to an online user experience. Many online classes are designed simply to mimic the experience of in-person learning, largely because facilitators and instructors haven't been given sufficient training or support in the theory and methods of online learning. Sadly, this lack of training and support has caused many learners and instructors alike to blame the online environment itself.

But it's not the fact of being online that's to blame for a crummy learning experience. It's a lack of attention to what people's experiences are like when they are online. It's a gap between an understanding of user experience design and actual learning design.

Designing for learning means designing an environment where users have clear choices. It means creating a space where learners can find what they need in the way that they need it and feel supported all along the way.

Design for Possibility

Learning is often associated with a stodgy, formal environment, like a schoolroom with desks bolted to the chairs. That's because learning, historically, is a lot about control: pour some ideas into learners' minds, and they'll come away with new knowledge. Paolo Freire famously critiqued this model, referring to it as the "banking model" of education, which assumes that learners are only there as vessels to receive and file away information (like depositing money in a bank).[1]

But in the last two to three decades, nearly ubiquitous access to the internet and mobile devices has provided platforms that give learners a lot more agency and control in where, when, how, and why they might engage with a learning experience. And while the technology itself hasn't disrupted "the banking model" of education, it certainly makes the deficits of the banking model all the more visible. You can try to force learners online to watch a bunch of videos with no engagement or follow-up. Or you can attempt to keep learners still and silent while staring into a web camera. But you're definitely not going to succeed. After all, it's all too easy to get distracted and find new and interesting things to do online. Online, learners are no longer at the mercy of what a teacher tells them to do; instead, they get to navigate through their own experiences because the technology does not keep them confined to one place at a time. If you really want someone to learn something online, it's important to keep them engaged and give them a reason why they should be there learning in the first place.

In today's world, successful online learning experiences put learners in the driver's seat. For example, Codecademy, an online learning platform founded in 2011, offers a large and growing catalog of courses in web design, machine learning, data science, and related subjects in coding languages and computer science. As of 2023, over 100,000 paid subscribers have used Codecademy to learn how to write code (see Figure 1.1).

---

1   Paolo Freire, *Pedagogy of the Oppressed* 30th anniversary edition, (New York: Bloomsbury Press, 2000. Originally published 1970).

FIGURE 1.1
The Codecademy course enables users to see the how, what, and why of an activity all at once by showing three key pieces of information for a user learning HTML for the first time: a description and purpose for the activity, the terminal for writing the code, and the rendering of what the HTML code produces for the web.

A typical lesson on Codecademy starts with a short introductory text explaining a concept or idea; in this case, how an HTML form works. Learners read through the explanation followed by step-by-step instructions describing the process to build a form. At each step, learners can click "Stuck? Get a hint." A concept review provides a sample "cheat sheet" that can be used to review the main concepts in the lesson, and learners can also check the community forms to see what questions other learners asked about the lesson. In the center window, learners can run and troubleshoot their code in real time, and on the right, they can view the visual output produced by the code (a mockup for a fictional business called *Dave's Burgers*).

Codecademy is one of many examples of digital learning platforms that have transformed the experience of learning in the past twenty years; others include LinkedIn Learning (formerly known as Lynda.com) created in 2002, Khan Academy in 2008, and Coursera in 2012. While these platforms have not replaced a lot of traditional learning experiences, they are designed in ways that give learners the agency to stop, start, pause, apply, and retry new concepts without the time constraints of a formal learning experience.

A Brief History of Online Learning

The seeds of online learning experiences were planted by the internet in the 1980s. Concurrently (in 1984), Malcolm Knowles, an adult learning theorist, created a theory of "andragogy" or "adult learning" that posited four key principles as critical to helping adults learn new ideas: having a strong self-concept, having a reservoir of prior learning experiences to draw upon, having a readiness to learn, and having an orientation to what it means to learn. These four principles, he argued, needed to be applied to the growing world of online training experiences, including the integration of a clear stated purpose for the learning experience, a task-oriented way of organizing content, the inclusion of varied learning activities, and room for learner agency and direction. These kinds of principles set the stage for the continued growth of online learning in the 1990s.

By the 1990s, online courses began to emerge, mostly centered on college campuses, often in states with large rural populations, like Utah, where students would have to travel long distances to attend class in a brick-and-mortar classroom space. Online classes grew steadily throughout the early 2000s and by 2011 about one-third of U.S. college students were taking at least one course fully online.

The flexibility and ease of accessing online learning experiences has continued to be facilitated by the growth in consumer technologies that make information even more portable and convenient to access. In 2007, Apple introduced the first iPhone and launched what has become a thriving ecosystem of digital learning. This growth in consumer technology has made the prevalence of learning experiences online all the greater; learners have to learn how to use their iPhones in order to continue buying and engaging with iPhones. As such, programs such as the Google Analytics Academy, the Meta Community Manager certification, HubSpot Academy, and the Salesforce Trailhead program are all growing and thriving consumer technology education programs, in large part because they count on a growing consumer base remaining interested in becoming better users and learners on the tools of a persistently growing consumer technology ecosystem. Smartphones are now used by many more learners than laptops or other large screens.[2] Even with

---

2 "Mobile Fact Sheet 2021," Pew Research Center, April 7, 2021, accessed March 21, 2023, www.pewresearch.org/internet/fact-sheet/mobile/

this unprecedented growth in access to online learning experiences, the need for theories like Freire's and Knowles' persisted; increased access did not necessarily mean an increased understanding of how to develop an experience that would really, truly be meaningful to learners.

The need for an immediately accessible learning experience became even clearer at the peak of the worldwide COVID-19 pandemic in March 2020. This catastrophic event forced many people into online learning because of "lockdowns" that prevented people from gathering in brick-and-mortar spaces. From early 2020 through the end of 2021, learning experiences across industries were rapidly spun into remote experiences. It's worth noting that the customer education industry, with companies such as Salesforce and HubSpot Academy leading the way, were leaders in developing online learning experiences prior to the pandemic. However, outside of the customer education industry, remote learning experiences were often considered "inferior" to an on-site class experience. But the experiences of emergency remote learning opened many trainers' and teachers' eyes to new possibilities for learning and gave a wider range of individuals more ubiquitous engagement with other learners.

The rapid rise of "emergency remote teaching" has been an earthquake in the lives of instructors and course designers, and the aftershocks continue today. There's no unwinding the clock on the experiences that lots of students and professionals alike had with learning online, and the key for learning designers now is to consider how, with deliberate time and planning, the tools for online learning can be designed to be even more attentive to users' needs. It's easy to anticipate that online learning will continue to grow because of the following criteria:

- **Accessibility:** People no longer need to travel to brick-and-mortar campuses or offices and can access learning from home or wherever they have access to a smartphone and a good internet. Plus, disabled learners have access to tools like closed captions and screen readers, which can ensure their access to the materials they need.

- **Social mobility:** Many people have either been priced out of continued learning opportunities, such as enrolling in higher education courses, or have not found traditional continued learning opportunities to meet their needs as full-time workers or caregivers. There is a growing need for people to learn outside of formal, inflexible, and expensive channels.

- **Career growth:** Learners today are often driven by a desire to change or advance in their careers. Technology drives many of these learners, who discover that they need specialized training to move up the career ladder.

This brief snapshot of the landscape of learning begins to explain why there is so much in motion now. Today's learners are seeking ways to learn at their own pace and on their own schedules. They want to learn in their own ways, gravitating toward interactive experiences to test and practice their learning, rather than learning primarily from textbooks or a long lecture.

Learning designers and others who create learning experiences face both huge opportunities and big challenges.

Why Learners Today Are a Different Kind of User

Learning experience design reflects a growing body of work that combines user-experience design (UX) with learning science. A learner is a special kind of user, with their own needs and values. If you want to check an account balance using your mobile banking app, you can log in, look up the balance, and you're done (if the app is working properly). If you want to learn how to design a website using semantic HTML, you need much more information. You need to learn how to learn.

Online learning platforms are complex information systems. Designing these systems draws upon several fields, including:

- **Information design (or information architecture):** A process for designing how users move through complex systems. Information design makes information both findable and understandable.
- **Instructional design:** A process for designing and developing learning experiences.
- **Learning science:** Theories and practices developed from neuroscience, psychology, and education research to inform how people learn.
- **Visual design and UI:** An understanding of how the visual layers of an online experience look and behave.

- **User research:** Research to learn about learners' needs and behaviors.

- **Content strategy:** A process for imagining and planning the content across the product or experience.

Language from these fields informs the planning, sketching, prototyping, and production of digital learning experiences.

A Model of Learning Experience Design

Learners are not sponges who absorb information through osmosis. But many learning platforms are unconsciously based on a model that defines learning as *information transfer*. Even formal courses often present learning as expertise being delivered directly from instructor to student. Current work in learning science and related fields suggests, however, that learning is an active process. Learners do not absorb knowledge; they actively create new knowledge.

That's why you need to design the learning experience with a specific learning experience design model in mind. The learning experience design model begins by centering on the learner. The learner's interactions with the instructor, course website or platform, learning activities, and other course materials to support the learners' practices combine to form the essential learning experience, as shown in Figure 1.2.

MAKING LEARNING EXPERIENCE DESIGN TRANSPARENT

Most educators agree that the best way to engage a learner from the start is to help them identify their experiences and motivations for taking the course. Andreina Parisi-Amon, the Vice President of Teaching and Learning for Engageli, an educational technology company, notes how important it is when designing a course experience to be "really direct with folks and give them the why and the expectations in terms of helping them see why it is that we're asking them to participate, what we expect them to gain from the experience." Being clear about the expectations and stating what learners can really expect from the experience makes the learning environment also feel safer. In Parisi-Amon's words, "That removes that surprise, and that also makes the learner understand why they're being asked to do something that pushes them to the edge of their current knowledge."

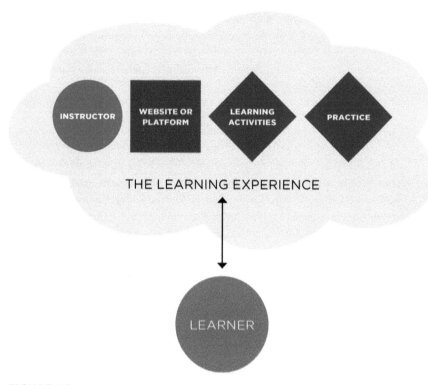

FIGURE 1.2

This user-centered learning experience design model demonstrates how the learner's behavior, motivation, and engagements with the course need to impact the course design just as much as the course design needs to impact and engage the learner.

The experience-design model defines learning as an active and interactive process. Instead of passively consuming information, as in a content-delivery model, the learner in this model is actively creating knowledge through a process of using, interacting with, and creating things. The learner is doing the work rather than the instructor.

This focus on the learner and their behavior in the experience design model happens not just through direct instructor-to-student feedback, but also through an automated framework. For example, in Duolingo, every time a user completes a lesson on the app, they receive automated acknowledgment of their progress and a score sheet detailing their performance, including the areas where they excelled and struggled. The next time the user logs in, they receive a customized set of lessons that are aligned with their progress report. So, if the user succeeds in lessons on using, say, modifiers in Spanish, they see lessons about modifiers less frequently. And if the user struggled with conjugating verbs in prior lessons, they see more lessons on verb conjugation, which will reinforce the user's need for practice in this area.

In the case of the automated language learning app, the user is getting real-time and automatic adjustments (feedback) based on their performance in the activities. This process is often referred to as an *individualized learning experience*. This kind of automation is not possible in all learning contexts, but this model of design centers the user in their experience and offers them materials that are aligned with their needs, at least as far as the robot understands them. In Chapter 11, "Reviewing Your Learning Experience," we'll explore the benefits and limitations of using robots or other forms of artificial intelligence for feedback.

We've found that many instructors tend to overemphasize the content of their courses, seeking that one perfect reading or that one perfect example that will enable them to get their point across to learners. In contrast, the experience design model encourages designers to focus on what the learners are doing—or how they are using the content and why.

This doesn't mean that content for learning can't be designed in an interactive way. But interaction is not the same thing as learning.

Peloton's instructional exercise content library is a perfect example. Peloton bike users get access to a novel range of exercise videos that they can play whenever they'd like, and they are incentivized to interact with those videos through several features. Exercisers can track their progress, earn badges for completing a certain number of workouts, and compete with other Peloton users on a live leaderboard to gamify their experience.

Where Peloton excels is by building a powerful community. Peloton users can identify "friends" to add to their accounts so that they can invite others to join rides with them and build accountability networks. This community helps users build strong motivation to take more classes and be in a community together. Most Peloton users don't expect to become professional athletes by purchasing access to the Peloton app or buying a Peloton bike. They want to build a habit by investing in a commitment, not developing mastery.

When users ride on a Peloton bike, they are not receiving feedback about how effective their form is on the bike. Rather, they are receiving instructions and incentives to keep them exercising. There are videos to help them set up the bike and strive for better form, but short of remaining uninjured, they may never really know for certain if they're riding the Peloton bike like a professional athlete. And that's OK! That's likely not their goal. But it's worth understanding and appreciating the difference. Building a habit and a motivation to learn are part of a learning experience. But without getting direct feedback on how to improve, learning isn't possible.

Interaction design and learning design are not the same thing.

If your end goal is to design training or a course that users will be incentivized to complete, then a gamified video playlist, like the Peloton app, may very well do the trick. However, if the end goal of your training or your course is for a learner to be able to apply that knowledge to a variety of flexible situations and gain new knowledge that you can assess for authentic learning, then your learning design is going to require some well-designed interventions.

A starting point for that intervention is remembering that you're designing for users who have specific needs. Knowing what those needs are and how you can optimize your design to meet those needs is the goal.

It's Not All About You

When you've given a presentation in front of a room, have you ever heard the advice to imagine that your audience is naked? It's a piece of advice that's meant to calm you down and make you laugh, but it's also advice that's communicating something important about presenting information: the more pressure you take off yourself to perform, the better.

Imagining your audience naked is about remembering that a presentation is not just about you. It's just as much about how you feel about the audience you're with as it is about how you're feeling in your own skin. And while imagining the audience naked is not advice that works for everyone, it remains popular and well-known precisely because it communicates something learning designers need to remember when leading or designing a learning experience: *it's not all about you.*

When you're leading and designing something, you're going to have an impact. But also remember how *you've* felt as a learner in a training or a class. You might have some vague memories of how the teacher or facilitator looked and acted. But what you probably remember most is how *you felt* taking that training or being in their class. Now that you're in the position of facilitating or designing a learning experience online, it's tempting to get hung up on how learners might perceive you or the content you've created. And while appearances *do* matter, they only really matter in one way: how those appearances impact how your learners will get what they need from the learning experience.

ENCOURAGING LEARNERS TO BRING THEIR WHOLE SELVES

Successful learning designers create a space where learners can bring their whole selves to the experience without fear of judgment or risk of exclusion or discrimination. This is difficult to achieve and is harder to accomplish in formal learning contexts where learners might not have natural or clear opportunities to share a personal story. But it's not impossible, especially if designers are willing to think creatively and with a clear understanding of the real people whom they're impacting.

Katherine Fisne, a senior eLearning architect at American Public University System, explains how when she works with educators, she recommends activating social-emotional elements of learning into every component of the course design. As an example, she recommends that every time a course includes something like a community discussion board where students have to submit an assignment, the assignment should also include an optional "fun" piece.

For example, in a discussion board assignment for a math class, some prompts ask students to share memes about math or write a haiku about their math class. And students will do it when they're invited! Educators should integrate the "fun" pieces with the "work" pieces, rather than separating them out. In Katherine's words, "We know that early engagement keeps someone in a course overall, so building that in early and often will help with concerns about the rigor or engagement with online classes."

Seeing Learners in 3D

The idea that you are *not* your learners has an important corollary: You need to design for real people—people who are *not* you.

Part of designing in 3D is recognizing the reality that learners are more diverse than you might think. You are probably already working with learners who have disabilities, for example. In fact, you can assume that about one-fifth of your audience is using some form of assistive technology to access and engage your content, from captions to screen readers. You are also probably working with learners who speak more than one language, and who may never have experienced learning in a way that's ever explicitly been designed for them.

Chances are, you are also designing for learners who are stressed and have other demands on what researchers call *cognitive load*. Designing with the goal of reducing cognitive load will make learning experiences easier for learners to process, absorb, and maintain their engagement.

Online learning requires an engagement of both mind and body. Designing for real people requires learning designers to understand and empathize with people who experience learning differently than they do across many dimensions.

Learning doesn't just happen to people. It's a designed experience that has defined goals and outcomes. If achieved, those goals and outcomes should evoke positive feelings for the learners. Defining how the goals and outcomes of the experience align with who the learners are is an important starting point for any learning experience design project.

Dr. Rob Rubalcaba, a mathematician at San Diego City College, was asked to contribute a series of practice problems to a mobile-friendly, online calculus course designed for learners who had previously had challenging experiences in math. Dr. Rob, as his students call him, knew that many of the learners who would enroll in the course came from a variety of cultural backgrounds, and many were Black, Latinx, or of mixed race. As such, he designed activities that made abstract mathematical concepts concrete with objects that he knew would have cultural significance for the students in the course.

When illustrating the concept of mapping a parabolic curve, Dr. Rob posted a photo of a tortilla that he had cut into six parts. For the activity, he asked the learners to do the same thing: go to their kitchen and get a tortilla, a pita, a pupusa, or a flatbread. He asked the learners to then cut their own tortilla-like object into six distinct pieces (he had clear instructions on where to make the cuts). He then informed the students that they would calculate the curvature of the tortilla and advised that they move the tortilla around as needed to help them see the differences in distance as part of their calculation.

The tortilla exercise shows how Dr. Rob anticipated a way that many learners might appreciate seeing an abstract concept illustrated. It's clearly not a technique that will work for everyone, but it's an effective combination of demonstrating cultural awareness while still advancing the content needed in the course. It would have been just as easy for Dr. Rob to identify a practice problem from a textbook to illustrate the notion of creating a parabolic curve. But instead, he chose to rethink the exercise so that learners could understand it experientially.

The Learning Design Process

Learning design is an *iterative* rather than a *linear* process. There are starting places for the learning designer, but those starting places may need to be returned to repeatedly to ensure that the vision for the learning experience is clear and that the needs of the learners are met. A learning designer may need to circle back, repeat steps, and return to earlier parts of the process multiple times (see Figure 1.3).

The steps of the learning design process are as follows:

- Learn more about who the learners are.
- Identify the main problem to solve for the learners.
- Define an endpoint: a vision for the learners at the end of the experience.
- Create a list of learning goals.
- Build a learning map around your list of learning goals.

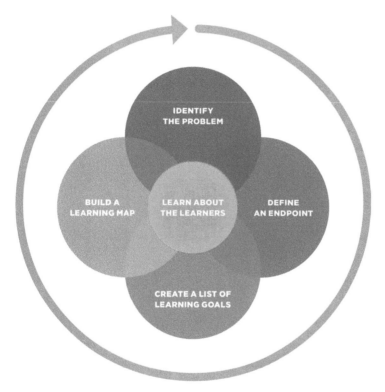

FIGURE 1.3

The learning design process illustrates the iterative nature of designing a learning experience, all while keeping learners' needs at the center of the design thinking process.

As a content designer you should assume that online learners will not follow the path you have laid out. Therefore, you must make it possible for them to determine their own ways through the content. The best way to understand how your learners will navigate your material is to build feedback loops and spaces for reflection and evaluation into your course or learning experience. (See Chapter 10, "Giving Your Learners Feedback.")

This learning design model is the foundation for launching an online course experience that keeps learner-centered needs in mind all the way through.

Takeaways

- **Build a full experience, not just content.** A meaningful learning experience is developed based on not just about *what* people are learning, but *how* they are learning.

- **Design with the possibilities of engaging online in mind.** Don't try to resist the multiple ways that learners can engage online. Lean into the options and design for experiences that can be accessed in multiple ways.

- **Design with purpose.** Know why your learners are engaging with your learning experience and remain aligned with that purpose as you begin your design process.

- **Keep diverse learner needs in mind.** Embrace the fact that learners will have different needs for your courses and anticipate what those needs are as you move forward.

- **Learning design is an iterative process.** There are steps you can follow from start-to-finish when engaging with the learning design process, but bear in mind that you may need to revisit and reengage with those steps as you develop your learning experience.

Learning About Your Learners

L earners often feel vulnerable and uncertain when learning something new. They may feel a whole range of emotions: challenged, angered, bored, excited, or curious. Accounting for this range of emotions as a learning designer is not easy. But when you're in the position of designing for a learning experience, it's important to remind yourself of what it feels like to learn. If you don't, you run the risk of designing experiences that may not resonate with your audience.

It's an impossible task to anticipate every person's feelings who will engage in your experience, of course. But it is very possible to imagine what learners might experience when they're taking the class that *you're* designing in particular.

Both of us began our teaching careers by teaching required writing classes for first-year college students. We could anticipate pretty quickly what the range of feelings would be for the learners in our classes: disgruntlement at having to take a required writing class, anxiety about having to write in an academic context, genuine curiosity about developing strong writing skills, and so on. We learned to design activities that would be attentive to this range of needs, knowing we couldn't respond to all these feelings all at once, but knowing they should be addressed explicitly along the way when possible.

The people that you're designing a course for fundamentally shape how you're going to create your course—from the vocabulary you use in your instructions to the types of images you choose to include. Different audiences have access to different pieces of knowledge, so they will reorient to what you're designing accordingly.

This chapter focuses on the prework that you'll do before the course design process even begins. Remember that learning about your learners is at the center of the course design model: what you can learn about who you're designing for should inform the remaining decisions you have to make about what goes into the course itself.

As a learning designer, it's important to seek constant feedback from people as part of your design process. That said, you may be designing a course on a tight time frame and may not have an opportunity to get as much user feedback as you'd like. This chapter offers a sequence of ideas to learn about your learners more carefully, starting with the steps you should absolutely take regardless of how quickly you're designing the course and ending with the steps that you could take if you have more time available to you. Each section in this chapter will give you some ideas of things you could do to learn about your learners in a particular sequence, but if you need to stop at the first set of steps, that's still better than doing nothing at all. Basically, the more you can learn, the more information you'll have to inform your course design. But if you can't do it all, that's OK, too. Try to approach learning design work with a spirit of curiosity, knowing that the more perspectives you can gather to inform your design process, the better.

Quick-Start Design Thinking Activity

Design thinking is a popular approach to problem-solving among entrepreneurs, engineers, and user researchers (see Figure 2.1). If you're on a short timeline to design a course and you need to get some ideas flowing quickly about who you're designing a course for, design thinking practices offer some good brainstorming exercises that can get your thoughts moving.

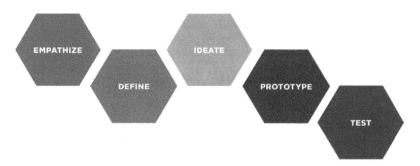

FIGURE 2.1

The design thinking process demonstrates how product designers can build new ideas by moving through a five-stage process: empathizing with the user, defining the need, ideating upon ways to respond to the need, prototyping the ideas, and then testing with end users.

The design thinking process developed at the Hasso Plattner Institute of Design at Stanford University (commonly known as the Stanford d.school) has a clear first step for understanding who your learners are: empathy. Specifically, design thinkers encourage designers to empathize with end users so that they can understand potential pain points, roadblocks, or challenges to using a particular product. From there, designers can use what they've learned from empathizing with their users to creating clear definitions for the problem they're trying to solve, ideating potential solutions, prototyping designs, and then testing those designs.

When it comes to learning design, the course itself is the closest thing to a "product" that's developed, but the key difference between the Stanford Design Thinking process and a learning design process is that the process is cyclical and iterative, especially when it comes to the "empathy" step and appreciating who the learners are in a particular class. That is, when you're learning about who your learners are for a class, your assumptions and understandings of them will continue to progress; your thinking does not end at the prototyping and testing stages.

When designing a course, designers can adapt a design thinking exercise called "How might we...?" for the empathize stage of the process.

- **As quickly as you can, write down three to five common problems that you anticipate a learner might have in your course.** These might be generic problems like an inability to turn in assignments on time or not being able to navigate the course website easily. Or they could be more specific problems that you've seen prior students experience if you've designed a similar kind of course before.

- **Look at your problems and try to rewrite the problems as "How might we?" questions.** Reframe your thinking about the problems that learners might experience into questions that you can try to answer with your learning designer. For example, if a problem you identified is "Not being able to navigate the course website easily," the concern could be reframed: "How might we make the course website easier to navigate?"

Finding answers to your three to five questions or problems can help you prioritize the key design choices for your learning experience in ways that were based on empathizing with and appreciating common learners' struggles. From there, it will be much easier (and much more research-informed) to conceptualize the rest of your online learning experience.

Ideal/Longer Timeline: Learner Persona Activity

With a longer timeline, consider taking some additional time to flesh out your understanding of who your learners are in your learning experience context. Constructing a persona is a common UX design approach for imagining and anticipating an end user's experiences. It typically involves creating a fictionalized biography of an imagined person with a mix of demographic details (such as age, gender, race, hometown, or other family members) and their anticipated needs, frustrations, or motivations for using the product that you're designing for. When you construct a persona in the context of building a learning experience, the goal is to keep the learner's primary needs at the forefront. It's an exercise in remembering: "What's in it for the learner when they take this course?"

User personas can help learning designers build empathy for their users (see Figure 2.2). If you haven't taken a course as a learner yourself in a long time, you may have forgotten what it's like to be a student. In building a persona, you have an opportunity to remember what it might feel like to be engaged in a learning experience. It also gives you an opportunity to imagine what other kinds of learners might experience when they're taking a class, and how it might feel for them to be in the vulnerable and scary position of learning something new. Think of building a persona as an invitation to put yourself in someone else's shoes and imagine how their life experiences may bring them into your learning context.

Remember that if you don't know what's "in it" for a learner beyond checking off a requirement or finishing a certification, you're going to have a hard time sustaining their interest and their motivation. As such, building a persona may give you some added essential insight into how your learner's experiences, motivations, frustrations, and concerns can shape the pacing and substance of the activities that you design.

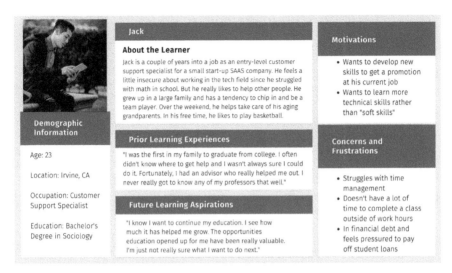

Jack

Demographic Information

Age: 23

Location: Irvine, CA

Occupation: Customer Support Specialist

Education: Bachelor's Degree in Sociology

About the Learner

Jack is a couple of years into a job as an entry-level customer support specialist for a small start-up SAAS company. He feels a little insecure about working in the tech field since he struggled with math in school. But he really likes to help other people. He grew up in a large family and has a tendency to chip in and be a team player. Over the weekend, he helps take care of his aging grandparents. In his free time, he likes to play basketball.

Prior Learning Experiences

"I was the first in my family to graduate from college. I often didn't know where to get help and I wasn't always sure I could do it. Fortunately, I had an advisor who really helped me out. I never really got to know any of my professors that well."

Future Learning Aspirations

"I know I want to continue my education. I see how much it has helped me grow. The opportunities education opened up for me have been really valuable. I'm just not really sure what I want to do next."

Motivations

- Wants to develop new skills to get a promotion at his current job
- Wants to learn more technical skills rather than "soft skills"

Concerns and Frustrations

- Struggles with time management
- Doesn't have a lot of time to complete a class outside of work hours
- In financial debt and feels pressured to pay off student loans

FIGURE 2.2

Creating a learner persona card can help learning designers create a concrete profile of who they anticipate might engage with their learning experience. This learner persona card includes information that illustrates an understanding of a learner's identity, motivations, concerns, frustrations, and aspirations.

Learner personas may include the following information:

- **Name**
- **Demographic Information (Description):** What is their background? Their age? Gender? Race? Cultural heritage?
- **Prior Learning Experiences:** What are their prior learning experiences like? How do these prior learning experiences shape how they'll experience your course or training?
- **Future Learning Aspirations:** What does this person want to learn more about, generally speaking? Where do they see areas of growth in their continuing education?
- **Motivations (or Purpose):** Why is this person taking the class you're designing? Why do they want to complete this course or training? To what extent is their motivation internal or external? How does their motivation to this class influence the ways that they might behave in your class or training context?
- **Concerns and Frustrations (Problems):** What concerns or frustrations does this person have with their learning? With the content or subject matter in your particular course or training?

AVOIDING COMMON PERSONA PITFALLS

Concern #1: Personas sometimes reproduce stereotypes. When UX designers try to construct personas about particular people (busy, working moms or hip, twenty-something city dwellers, or senior citizens uncomfortable with technology adoption), it's very easy to reproduce stereotypes that may be useless at best and quite harmful at worst.

Solution: Focus on the typical "pain points" your course attempts to solve, and use those to consider how different people might respond or be engaged in your course. That way, you can avoid problematic stereotypes that could mislead or impact your design. You can also increase your exposure to diverse people by asking for input on building these personas from colleagues, friends, or family. Treat your research and discovery stages iteratively: keep developing and thinking about people all the way through, and revise as you continue to discover more.

Concern #2: Personas can include too much information that doesn't guide the design process effectively. UX personas can dive deeply into fictional backstories, from the existence of siblings to the listing of hobbies or favorite books and video games. Some of this information may be useful for understanding your learners: understanding hobbies, for example, could give the learning designer insight into real-world examples that could inform or illustrate abstract learning concepts in a given course. However, extraneous details in a persona can be distracting, misleading, or a poor use of time to construct.

Solution: Think about what personal details in a learner's life could have a meaningful impact on what a learning designer could do. How might knowing someone's favorite books or video games inform your course design, for example? Perhaps anticipating that a lot of learners in the class could enjoy, say, zombie movies might help you design a unit with a horror movie theme.

Concern #3: Personas may be guided too much by one demographic detail rather than a holistic picture into their journey. A persona may, by the very nature of the exercise, reduce real humans down to flat caricatures that are artificially overly influenced by isolating age, race, gender, or some other detail or imagined experience.

Solution: When constructing motivations or problems for the personas, keep intersectionality in mind, understanding that no one's orientation to an experience is shaped solely by isolating age, race, or gender. This will only deepen the potential for interesting and diverse design decisions down the road.

With More Time: Surveys and Focus Groups

If you've got a long timeline to develop a course and you want to learn as much as you can about who you're supporting in the learning experience, you may want to consider some more rigorous learner research approaches. This may be especially useful if you're designing several courses for one group of learners. That way, all of the effort you put into researching the particular population of learners you're working with can impact the development not just of a single course, but of multiple related courses.

If possible, contact your students before the course, because this approach demonstrates to your learners that you're interested in seeking their needs and feedback as an audience right away. Whole books have been written about research methodologies for understanding an audience and their needs, so this section is going to provide only the most basic of tips to get started with user research methods that can inform your early course development and design.

Bear in mind that the recommendation to create surveys at the beginning of your course design process should be considered in conjunction with distributing some informal survey instruments or feedback-gathering mechanisms throughout the course experience itself. Ideally, the learning facilitator will want to check in with learners shortly after the experience has begun, in order to gauge learners' processes and experiences early on. It's also a good idea to check in on your learners at the midpoint of the learning experience to see how things are going for them while they're taking the course. We'll return to strategies for collecting learner feedback about their course experience in Chapter 11, "Reviewing Your Learning Experience."

For now, however, this section will remain focused on strategies and research approaches for learning about your learners in the spirit of ensuring that you're clearly aligned on their needs, expectations, attitudes, and ideas about online learning experiences.

Why Learner Surveys?

Surveys are a great tool to give learning designers an "at-a-glance" view of who your learners are and how they approach the online learning experience. Because learners' experiences with online learning may be particularly varied, catching some of the concerns early may help you avoid some common pitfalls in making learners feel disengaged, disconnected, or disinterested.

Your goal is to use your survey responses as an opportunity to catch areas of disconnect between learners' expectations and the learning design. Surveys are generally designed to:

- **Offer aggregated data about learner demographics.** Surveys can tell you how many different kinds of learners are enrolled in your learning experience so that you have a clearer sense of where your learners come from, how old they are, and what their gender and racial breakdown is.

- **Provide aggregated data about your learners' motivations for or interests in engaging in the learning experience.** Well-designed multiple-choice questions can give you some clear answers as to what motivated your learner to enroll in the course. For example, a survey could include a "yes" or "no" question about whether a learner was enrolled for a requirement or not.

- **Quantify feedback about learners' expectations before they start the course.** As a designer, it can be helpful for you to know several key metrics related to learners' expectations. For example, survey questions might ask learners how many hours they expect to spend taking the course or how much time they expect to interact with the instructor or their peers.

- **Provide a space for learners to share additional comments or perspectives.** Surveys are a good way to signal to learners that you are seeking feedback. Even if learners choose not to share any written feedback, they have the space to provide and convey comments anonymously.

For example, here are some questions to ask learners before the course begins, in order to discover more about them:

- On a scale of 1 to 4, how would you rate your prior online learning experiences?

- On a scale of 1 to 4, how would you rate your prior face-to-face or in-person learning experiences?

- Which of the reasons below (from a multiple-choice list) best aligns with your reasons for taking this course?

Responses to these questions can give you a better sense of what kinds of attitudes and experiences your learners will generally bring to their learning experience. They may help you anticipate what specific resources to create or design in the course development process.

Tips for Designing Surveys

A survey's results are only as good as their questions. If you design your survey with questions that are confusing, misleading, or biased, your results will also be confusing, misleading, and biased. You want to ensure that your answers are as clear as possible in order to inform your design. When you're designing survey questions, keep these items in mind:

- **Keep your questions neutral.** Do not ask "leading" questions or questions that may reveal your own biases about a particular topic. For example, instead of asking "Why is taking this class so important to you? Select all that apply." Ask: "What are your motivations for taking this class? Select all that apply."

- **Use language that most people can understand.** You don't want your learners to be deterred by language that is too technical or complex. A good rule of thumb is to ask questions using language that you can assume most people will understand. If you're not sure if the language in your survey is general enough, consider showing your survey questions to someone who doesn't work with you, like a friend or a family member. For example, instead of asking "Which of the metacognitive goals below aligns with your motivation for taking this course?" ask: "Which of these common goals best aligns with your motivation for taking this course?"

- **Consider the impacts of different question types on your learner's time.** Some survey question types will require greater thinking than others. For example, matrix questions, where users have to align a factor in a column with a different factor in a row, can require more thought than a simple multiple-choice question. While a matrix-style question may be appropriate if you want your user to make comparisons, consider whether the complexity is worth your user's time.

- **Use open-ended questions sparingly.** Open-ended questions require the most intensive time commitment from your users. Try to limit these questions as much as possible and prioritize where you really need to hear directly from your users. Remember that if you're looking for a story or a personal insight, a survey is probably not the right tool for you to use. Surveys are primarily for looking at aggregations of responses, not for getting deep insights.

- **Use a consistent rating scale.** If you are having your learners rate anything on a numbered scale (for example, "on a scale of 1 to 5..."), use the same scaling system throughout the entire survey. It will be confusing for your users if you are switching between different sets of numbered scales, because they will likely lose track of what each of the different scales means and may misinterpret the value of the scaled response they're entering.

- **Ask for one thing at a time.** Some survey questions can be double-barreled and may ask for users to consider more than one thing at a time. When you ask for more than one response in a question, you will not receive clear answers to your question anyway. For example, instead of asking "Do you anticipate that this course will help you achieve personal and professional goals?" ask "Do you anticipate that this course will help you achieve professional goals?"

- **Keep your survey as short as possible.** Your learner's time is valuable. Prune down your questions as much as you can. When you're first drafting your survey, you may come up with a long list of questions. This is a good starting point. Eventually, aim to include a maximum of 10 questions on your survey so that you can keep response time limited to a few minutes.

Your survey will likely require revision and review. Show your survey to as many people as possible before you distribute it to your learners so that you can get as much feedback as possible on how clear, concise, and easy it is for people to take and understand the survey.

Tips for Distributing Surveys

Typically, a learning designer will know who has enrolled in the experience prior to the start. A survey could be sent to that roster of individuals to give the designer a bit more nuanced perspective about who is in the course prior to its start. When you distribute a survey, let your students know that the survey is optional and anonymous. By keeping the survey anonymous, you guarantee safety when the learners share their responses without identifying information. Bear in mind that the purpose of a precourse survey is to get a general sense of the learners' experiences and feelings, not to get individualized responses, so honoring anonymity can get you some more honest answers.

You don't want students to feel coerced into sharing feedback or feel resentment about divulging information. There is already a power differential at play between the learning facilitator/designer and the learner. Namely, the learner is dependent upon the facilitator or designer to assess their work and to determine whether they've completed the course successfully. When you give the learners more choices about completing a survey, you've acknowledged this power differential and given some control back to them.

There may be some situations where students need to disclose personal information. So, as you distribute your survey, mention that if the students have questions or requests that require an instructor response, they should communicate with the instructor directly to share any concerns they may have. Specifically, if a learner wishes to disclose a disability accommodation or other similar, personal concerns that may impact their ability to participate in the learning experience, they should be sure to do so outside of the anonymous survey.

Given the low-stakes nature of a precourse survey, you may want to send one to two reminders after you send the initial survey out. It's easy for people to ignore surveys. Reminders may improve your response rate while signaling that you're interested in checking in with learners throughout the course experience (see Chapter 9, "Building Connections Among Learners," for a deeper discussion of learner check-ins).

Tips for Using Survey Feedback

After you've received responses to your survey, you'll probably be simultaneously overwhelmed and excited about all the information available to you. Start by looking for trends that may inform your framing of course content. One of the most valuable pieces of information you can learn from your survey is the background of your learners. Knowing more about their ages, their years of prior education, or their motivations may compel you to make different decisions about how you present information in your learning experience.

Look for response patterns that may inform the amount of content that you include in your course. For example, it might be useful for you to know, based on the survey responses, how much time your students will be able to put in to the course you're designing on average. The average amount of time your students can spend on the course can help inform the length and rigor of the course you're designing. While you may have some limitations and requirements for what you're supposed to include, you may reconsider the pacing, the number of activities, or the amount of time commitment required based on the responses.

You're going to see outlier responses, but don't worry about those. The purpose of the survey is to focus on how the majority of respondents are going to experience your course. If you want to learn about more individualized responses or concerns, you can design a non-anonymized survey during the course itself where those individual voices can be heard.

Why Focus Groups?

Surveys will not give you the fullest view into your learners' prior experiences, attitudes, and expectations for online learning. In user research, researchers tend to use focus groups as a way to take a deeper dive into learner stories. In focus groups, researchers gather multiple users into the same space at the same time and ask them to answer a series of questions. The questions tend to be open-ended so that the users present can tell personal stories or build off of each other's experiences to inform the researcher's understanding of a particular topic or research question.

In the context of learning design, focus groups are useful for:

- Hearing individualized stories about prior learning experiences.
- Allowing learners to hear from each other and to generate feedback for the learning designer based on their peers' insights.
- Generating a conversation about desires, motivations, and frustrations with learning experiences.

The kinds of nuanced stories you may get from a focus group can be invaluable for anticipating problems in your design up front. In all likelihood, you may only be able to organize these groups once the course is in motion or after the course is over. Still, if you can create opportunities for dialogue with learners about their experiences, the information you glean will be more valuable.

Using Focus Groups to Check In

While it's certainly ideal to get as much information about your learners as you can before a course begins, it isn't always realistic. Therefore, if you want to get deeper insights beyond surveys into what learners want or need from the course, you might consider organizing some small "check-in" groups, which can be modeled after focus groups, during the first or second week of the course.

If your course experience is only a day or two long, this approach is probably not the right fit. But if you're working with a course that has a longer timeline or trajectory, making space to learn about your learners' experiences at the start of a term can go a long way toward helping you tweak and shape design choices during the course itself. It's worth thinking about early on how you'll learn enough about your learners to create an experience that's worthwhile for them.

Example questions for a check-in group during the first week of the learning experience might include:

- What makes you feel included in an online learning experience?
- What's an example of a time that an online learning experience worked really well for you?
- What contributed to your positive online learning experience?
- What's an example of a time that an online learning experience went poorly for you?
- What contributed to the negative online learning experience?

These questions can yield valuable stories about your learners' experiences that will help humanize your understanding of what effective learning design could look like. The responses to these questions may not be able to reshape your course dramatically—since it will already be in motion by the time that you conduct a first "check-in"— but the answers can inform small modifications and help you build the next course that you'll design.

Takeaways

- **Become a learner yourself.** Seek feedback constantly from people as part of the design process.
- **Use design thinking.** Write down three to five common problems that you anticipate a learner might have in your course.
- **Create learner personas.** Build empathy for the learners you are building your course for.
- **Create surveys.** Identify concerns that could make learners feel disengaged, disconnected, or disinterested in the online learning experience you're developing.
- **Lead focus groups when possible.** Listen to individualized stories about prior learning experiences and use that evidence to inform your design choices moving forward.

CHAPTER 3

Setting the Foundation

W hat is the course about?

This is probably the first question you'll be asked when designing a learning experience. But for a learning designer, even more important than the subject matter are the *outcomes* of the learning experience. Namely, the following:

- What skills will the learner develop?
- What practices will the learner become proficient in?
- What core concepts should the learner understand by the end of the course?

Some learning designers may be content experts. Others will not be. Regardless of what the designer knows about the subject matter, they should have a clear sense of the new knowledge, skills, and ideas that they want the student to develop by the end of the learning experience.

To set the foundation in a course, the first step is to figure out the endpoint of the course. This endpoint should be directly related to the problem being solved in the learning design. By keeping the end goals of the course in mind, the designer can think about what kinds of activities guide their learners from one step to the next until they complete the learning experience.

Starting from the end of the course is often referred to as *backward design*. Backward design is a process used to create and organize learning materials that can guide learners through the material. In conventional "forward" design, the designer begins with activities designed to teach the content of the learning, builds assessments to measure the learner's success, and finishes with making connections from the assessments to the learning goals of the course.[1] By reversing the usual order of the steps, backward design puts the learner and the learning process front and center. The goal in backward design is to intentionally start with well-defined overall goals for the learner.

---

1 Grant Wiggins and Jay McTighe, *Understanding by Design*, 1st ed. (Alexandria, VA: Assn. for Supervision and Curriculum Development, 1998).

Whether you're designing a course in two days, two weeks, two months, or longer, having a clear sense of the end goal for the course is the single greatest thing you can do to design a successful learning experience. That goal will be the foundation for everything else that you have to build.

Identify the Problem

Next, identify the main problem you are trying to solve for your learners, in order to define your endpoint goals. Sometimes the main problem is apparent and easy to identify. More often, you will find multiple, overlapping problems of different types. If you took some time to identify your learners' needs (see Chapter 2, "Learning About Your Learners"), you've probably identified a problem based on your knowledge and understanding of your learners already. The more you know about your learners, the more confident you will feel about your ability to identify and define their problems and needs.

Let's use the example of designing a course for survivors of strokes who want to learn how to recover and find calmness and stability. A list of problems that a designer might anticipate for their students could be the following:

- A middle-aged woman who has recently had a stroke for the first time in her life and is feeling scared about reentering the world and taking risks.

- A man over the age of 65 who has had a stroke within the past month and is feeling alone in his recovery experience.

- Someone who has had multiple strokes and is looking for more support from other survivors.

- Someone who recovered from a stroke many years ago, but wants to be reminded of effective coping strategies.

There could be many more problems than this (and a designer is not going to be able to anticipate them all). But starting to brainstorm the range of concerns that learners may face can be important for prioritizing what the learner might value and appreciate in the course.

Types of Learning Problems

Learning problems take many forms, and it is not always easy to sort them into clear categories. Often, you will find a problem of knowledge (learners need to know more about a topic, for example) that turns out to be a problem of process and skills (learners need more practice to develop their skills). Knowledge problems are usually "what" problems: What do learners need to know? Skill problems are usually "how" problems: How can learners develop mindfulness skills? Sometimes, one problem is closely related to another. Once you have a working list of the most important problems you want to focus on for your learners, you can sort them into groups similar to these:

- **Knowledge:** Learners need new knowledge to move ahead. Learning designers need to know what their learners already know, as well as what new things they need to know in order to progress. Sometimes learners' prior knowledge interferes with something new they need to learn. For example, students might need to move to a new software system, but their prior knowledge could get in the way.

- **Mindset and motivation:** Learners often struggle with mindset (they don't believe they can improve) or motivation (they don't want to do the work). Virtually every learning designer wrestles with these problems. Providing information (knowledge) and opportunities for practice (skills) also helps give motivation to your students.

- **Process and skills:** Students need to know how to do something (process), and they need opportunities to practice (skills).

- **Context and environment:** Learners need a supportive and well-defined context for learning. Learning designers can work to create an environment of sharing and collaboration, and can build context and culture around the process of learning.

Table 3.1 gives some examples of what it looks like to identify learning problems. Specifically, we'll continue to explore the example of designing a course to support stroke survivors. In this case, then, Table 3.1 maps out the kinds of problems that learners may have in the course to support stroke survivors and it identifies what types of problems the learners in that class may be experiencing. Seeing these problems in context can help clarify the definitions of the problems that learners may experience so that it's easier to identify design solutions later.

TABLE 3.1 MAPPING LEARNING PROBLEMS

Problems	Types of Learning Problems
Learners are stressed because they are having a hard time communicating after having a stroke.	Mindset and motivation: Your learners are having difficulties with verbal communication, which creates stress and frustration.
Learners know a little about mindfulness but want to learn more.	Knowledge: Learners need more information about what mindfulness is and how it helps to reduce stress.
Learners report that they have trouble maintaining a meditation routine.	Skills, motivation: Learners need skills for meditation, opportunities for practice, and support to create new routines.
Learners need support to use mindfulness techniques to reduce stress.	Context, skills: You can build an environment to support your learners, as well as opportunities for practice.

Anticipating Problems Unique to Online Learning

Online learners are often working adults. They take online classes specifically because they don't want to quit their jobs, and they see online classes as a solution to the problem of maintaining a job while seeking continued education. According to *U.S. News World and Report* data from 2017, the average age of a student seeking a Bachelor's Degree online is 32 years old, although average ages may vary for online learning experiences across industries and contexts.[2] In this case, an online learner may want to solve a problem related to stagnant career advancement.

Online learners may also seek online education to solve a personal problem. For example, they may be immunocompromised and unable to spend long periods of time around other people without concern for their personal health and safety. As such, online courses can help them solve the problem of advancing their education, career, and interests without needing to put their health at risk.

2 Jordan Friedman, "U.S. News Data: The Average Online Bachelor's Student," *U.S. News and World Report,* April 4, 2017, www.usnews.com/higher-education/online-education/articles/2017-04-04/us-news-data-the-average-online-bachelors-student

ASK QUESTIONS TO IDENTIFY PROBLEMS

If you have a limited amount of time, start by using a short list of questions about your learners. These questions will help you identify the main problems your learners are having. Their problems will generally cluster around four main types of problems: mindset and motivation, knowledge, skills, and environment. Then you can brainstorm some questions for each type of problem.

Here are some guiding questions to help you get started (see Table 3.2).

TABLE 3.2   IDENTIFYING COMMON LEARNING PROBLEMS

Problem Types	Brainstorming Questions	Problems Identified (in Stroke Recovery Class Example)
Mindset and Motivation	What are my learners resisting?	Learners are resisting trying new ways to practice mindfulness in their daily lives. They have an ingrained idea that they are "bad at meditating."
Knowledge	What do my learners need to know?	Learners really don't know a lot about mindfulness meditation, and what they do know may be based in misunderstandings.
Skills	Which skills do my learners need to practice?	Meditation is really challenging work, so learners need to sit with and practice meditation to develop the skill.
Environment	What is missing from my learners' environment?	The community of practitioners is missing. Learners may feel very much alone in practicing meditation and may lose interest or motivation because they don't have other people in their environment who are going through the same things that they are.

The COVID-19 pandemic that began in March 2020 exposed learners of all ages and life circumstances to the experience of accessing learning experiences remotely. So, online learners may also simply be learners who found value in their experiences of engaging in learning remotely during the pandemic and who are eager to keep their learning experiences online.

Knowing some of the underlying problems that may drive people online can help designers better align their learners' personal problems with the problems that arise in the context of a particular subject. If a designer knows that most of the learners in the class may be trying to work and learn at the same time, the designer will want to consider what kinds of problems may arise for students who are trying to do the course in small bursts of time in between work, family life, and other obligations.

Anticipating problems will also help designers anticipate needs related to retention. For many learners, the online environment itself can create problems that need to be addressed in your design. If you are producing videos, for example, recognize that some learners may have accessibility issues or simply resist viewing a lot of video content. Video can be very powerful and useful, but video is also a high-bandwidth item for your learners, both literally and figuratively. Some people may lack access to high-speed internet and others may find videos to be cognitively exhausting. Make sure that your videos are captioned and allow learners to use transcripts or other text equivalents for video content.

Once you've fully addressed the potential problems around online learning access points, you can start to brainstorm the alignment between learner problems, learner contexts, and learner goals.

Define an Endpoint

Defining an endpoint is a way to imagine where you want your learners to be at the end of the experience. A "learning endpoint" is a way to envision an overall goal or state. If you think of the learner's experience in terms of a journey, where does that journey end? An endpoint may not be literally a point: it can also be a state of mind or a condition. Some learning journeys may have a distinct endpoint; others may be more of a description of qualities or skills that learners will possess by the end of their learning.

WRITE AN ENDPOINT STATEMENT

An endpoint statement is a representation of what your learners should think or be able to do when they reach the end of your course or learning experience. This statement is an important way to capture your vision for the learners at the end of their journey. Defining these solutions and crafting an effective endpoint is a critical step in the process of designing the learning experience.

Here is a first draft of an endpoint statement for the stroke recovery class: "Learners in my course will be able to communicate in stressful situations. They will be able to use mindfulness skills in their daily lives to reduce stress. Learners will be able to share with others in the course to build trust and develop a daily meditation practice."

Your list of problems will give you a good start on the process of defining a learning endpoint. The goal here is to define where you want your learners to be at the end of the learning journey. Imagine that your learners have successfully completed your course. If you have described the problems that learners face at the beginning, you are in a good position to define their solutions. Crafting a description of where you want learners to be at the end of the learning journey will probably take several tries.

Create Your Learning Goals

Learning designers are often encouraged to start designing a new course with a list of learning goals. By defining learning goals, you can then move on to organizing a learning experience around those goals. You may find, though, that you get stuck and have to backtrack because your goals may be too abstract or removed from the real context.

Defining and writing useful learning goals takes practice. To be effective, learning goals need to present a short list of things that learners need to know and are able to do by the end of the course. There is no magic number for listing learning goals, but generally fewer are better. Three well-defined goals are usually better than seven goals that are too broad.

DRAFT AND REVISE YOUR LEARNING GOALS

Doing a deep rewrite of the goals for your class will enable you to sharpen your focus and improve your learners' ability to achieve the goals. In a first draft, you are likely to write learning goals that will be too big or too broad. As you revise them, try to define more succinctly what you really want your learners to be able to do. (See Table 3.3 for an example revision of broad learning goals.)

TABLE 3.3 IMPROVING LEARNING GOALS

Learning Goals	Revised Goals	Notes
Learners will be able to use mindfulness techniques in their daily lives.	Learners will be able to use breathing, guided audio meditations, and self-reflection to relieve stress in their daily lives.	The broad term "mindfulness techniques" has been revised to list discrete activities. The purpose is clearly defined, "to relieve stress."
Learners will be informed about the basic principles and techniques of mindfulness.	Learners will be able to explain how they use mindfulness techniques in their daily lives.	Be careful about words like "explain." Do you really want learners to *explain* or rather to *use* these techniques?
Learners will build a meditation practice or routine.	Learners will create a weekly plan for meditation practice.	This revised goal is more realistic and precise.
Learners will be able to share ideas and techniques with each other in the course.	Learners will meet weekly with a partner to share their progress in the course.	The revised goal is more practical and well-defined.

WEAVE LEARNER VALUES INTO
THE COURSE GOALS

What a designer wants learners to get out of the course may not
necessarily be in alignment with what the learners themselves
most value or appreciate about the course. Katherine Fisne, a
senior eLearning architect at American Public University, noticed
that when she designed and taught a statistics course, she wanted
students to be able to conduct complex statistical analyses by
the time the course was over. However, she noticed that what
students cited as their most valuable experience in the class was
learning how to use a piece of statistical software that they could
use in other academic or professional contexts later.

While Katherine's course outcomes didn't change as a result
of this information, she decided to build in content each week
throughout her course that asked students to engage with the
statistical software they found useful, even as she was keeping the
course about teaching statistical analysis at the forefront. When
she starts to design courses, Katherine asks herself, "What do I
think students are going to value about this learning experience?
At the end of this course, what do I think students will remember?"

Build a Learning Map

A learning map brings together all of the preceding steps in the
process and serves as a plan for designing and building your learning experience. A learning map connects the first three steps in the
learning design process: the main problem or problems to be solved,
the learner endpoint, and a list of learning goals.

In our example of building a mindfulness course for individuals
recovering from a stroke, we started with a list of the specific needs of
learners in that course. This list of needs created an understanding of
the problems that learners in the course faced. These problems led, in
turn, to a draft of an endpoint statement and a list of learning goals.
With this map in Table 3.4, we were well-prepared to build the course.

TABLE 3.4 MOVING FROM PROBLEMS TO LEARNING GOALS

Problems	Endpoints (Solutions)	Learning Goals
Learners are stressed because they are having a hard time communicating after having a stroke.	Learners in my course will be able to communicate in stressful situations. They will be able to use mindfulness skills in their daily lives to reduce stress. Learners will be able to share with others in the course to build trust and to develop a daily meditation practice.	Learners will be able to use breathing, guided audio meditations, and self-reflection to relieve stress in their daily lives.
Learners know a little about mindfulness but want to learn more.		Learners will be able to explain how they use mindfulness techniques in their daily lives.
Learners report that they have trouble maintaining a meditation routine.		Learners will create a weekly plan for meditation practice.
Learners need support to use mindfulness techniques to reduce stress.		Learners will meet weekly with a partner to share their progress in the course.

Creating Course Landmarks

If you're going to a new place for the first time, you'd probably start by looking at a map to get a general sense of where your new destination is located. The learning map is that first step: the map will give you, as the designer, a broader sense of how learners will get from Point A to Point B in your course. Yet, if you're trying to drive to a new place, knowing roughly where the destination is located will not be quite enough to get there. You'll need some detailed instructions, ideally a step-by-step guide that will help you successfully navigate from Point A to Point B.

That's the next step in your learning design process: creating those landmark stops in your learning map to stay on track and reach your end destination successfully. That means that in addition to establishing the problem, the endpoint, and the learning goals, you'll also want to indicate:

1. When certain instructional activities could happen to help reach the goals.

2. When and what kinds of evaluations or assessments of the learning could occur to provide evidence that the learner endpoint is achieved.

To build in the activities and assessments, you need to split apart your map problem-by-problem. Certain activities and assessments will be useful for solving some problems—and reaching your end-point in some situations—but not others. So, going into finer-grained detail about how you'll achieve certain problems and not others will also let you prioritize which learning activities and content pieces you need to design for which sections of the course. See our examples in Tables 3.5 and 3.6 to see how a map can be created over two full weeks of our example course.

TABLE 3.5 WEEK/UNIT 1: INTRODUCTION TO MEDITATION

Learning Goals and Dates	Activities	Evaluations	Tools
Learners will be able to use breathing, guided audio meditations, and self-reflection to relieve stress in their daily lives. Dates: 8/15–8/17	Listen to a guided audio meditation. Respond to a discussion forum post about the experience of listening to the guided audio meditation. Join for a live session to discuss the experience of using the guided meditation.	Mark forum responses for completion.	YouTube for audio meditation clip. Learning management system for discussion forum tool. Zoom for live session.
Learners will be able to explain how they use mindfulness techniques in their daily lives. Dates: 8/18–8/22	Create a self-recorded video introduction with a 2-minute overview of what "mindfulness" means to you. Watch a short video with Tara Brach on mindfulness philosophy. Take a short quiz on video takeaways. Read a short article by the Dalai Lama on meditation and its history.	Create automated responses for video quizzes. Write brief personalized feedback responses to intro videos.	YouTube for video clip. PDF editor or social annotation tool for online article.

TABLE 3.6 WEEK/UNIT 2: BUILDING A MEDITATION HABIT

Learning Goals and Dates	Activities	Evaluations	Tools
Learners will create a weekly plan for meditation practice. Dates: 8/23–8/26	Learners will complete a calendar within a graphic organizer to illustrate their weekly plan.	Written plans will simply be evaluated for completion.	Google Docs or Microsoft Word
Learners will be able to explain how they use mindfulness techniques in their daily lives. Dates: 8/29–8/31	Learners will complete a reflection journal assignment to describe what they've learned and how their learning will impact their practice.	Reflection journals will simply be evaluated for completion.	Google Docs or Microsoft Word

Mapping out the sequencing of activities and assessments in alignment with learning goals should help you, as the designer, see what gaps there may be in the organization of content and in terms of overall coverage in the course.

The Art and Science of Timing Activities

Sequencing activities is an important step for one of the more challenging aspects of learning design: estimating time on task. Different people work, think, and engage at different paces, so while it might not be possible to know exactly how long it might take the average person to complete the learning experience you're designing, it is possible to design a course in such a way that learners can anticipate timing needs and pace themselves accordingly

Establish Patterns

Consistency is key in an online learning experience. If there are certain activities that you know learners will need to do repeatedly in your online learning experience, try to have those activities happen in the same sequence. If you sequence the same activities in the same way in each week or in each discrete unit of your course, learners will be able to see the pattern and establish some clear expectations as a result. Once they have those expectations in place, they can estimate their time on task accordingly.

As an example, one sequence that you might try is called: "Watch, Reflect, Read, Respond, Try." In each weekly sequence, you'd create a pattern where the learner watches a video or listens to a podcast and then has to reflect, either by responding to a quiz or writing a response. (See Figure 3.1 as another example of this concept in action.) After that, the learner could take a deeper dive: they read a short article and then respond to the article, either by annotating it, recording an audio memo with their thoughts, or by taking a short quiz. Finally, they would finish out the sequence by "trying out" the learning for themselves in some form of evaluation, whether that's something like a test or the production of a project.

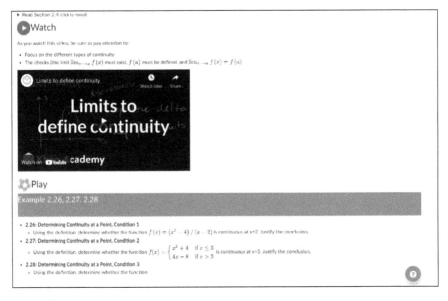

FIGURE 3.1

This online calculus course developed by Alexandria Rockey at Bakersfield College and Rob Rubalcaba at San Diego City College demonstrates the creation of a pattern on each page with learning content. Each of the sections consistently includes one of these headers to indicate what the learner will do with the content.

Create Themes for Each Section

There should be a variety of discrete topics that divide up the sequencing in your course (as modeled in the learning map). Consider giving each of these units a "theme" or topic that allows learners to see how one idea sequences into the next. This practice will also enable them to see how the topics for the course transition from one week to the next. Understanding how major themes move and evolve from week-to-week will also provide them with a clearer understanding of how their knowledge will progress throughout the course.

Provide Estimated Time on Task

While each person in the learning experience will likely have very different needs for their learning experiences, try to offer an estimate for how long it should take them to complete different parts of the learning sequence (see Figure 3.2). It could be as simple as including assignment instructions with an estimated amount of time for completion, particularly within a range, if possible. Try to overestimate the amount of time on task, rather than underestimate. That way, you're considering the upper-most range for time when applicable.

Step 1. Go to the "Peer Reviews" link in this assignment and locate the links to your group members' drafts.

Step 2. Read one of your group member's essays, leaving comments directly in the body of the paper itself. You will see commenting tools when you open up their essay. You can use the highlighting tool and the "comment" tool to add marginal feedback. At this stage, focus on CONTENT, not grammar. *Some focus on style at this stage may be useful for navigating the writer's address to the target audience and the genre for the composition.*

Because this piece is significantly longer than the proposal, you should aim to leave **at least 8-10 substantial comments within the margins of the essay** that point out things you really liked about the paper as well as instances where you got confused or felt that the writer was diverging from their overall point. Also, work towards answering the author's questions about their work; you want to be sure to address their interests.

Step 3. Complete the rubric on the right-hand side of the screen after you finish reading the proposal. Please provide a brief comment alongside each rubric item you've marked to explain your choice. Even if you marked the criterion as excellent, explain "why" you thought the author excelled at that criterion. **If the rubric crashes or you're unable to complete the rubric, you have the option to use the rubric simply as a guide (rather than as something that's "mandatory" to complete).**

Step 4. Offer a brief comment at the end with any final comments or questions you have for the author

**It should take approximately 30 minutes to read, provide marginal feedback, and complete the rubric for EACH peer's paper.*

Step 5. Repeat steps 1-4 for the other member of your peer review group.

FIGURE 3.2

This simple example from a writing course offers a clear estimation of time on task, broken into various, discrete steps.

Orient Your Learners to the Experience

In an online course, learners will come in with a variety of expectations about what the experience will be like. As a designer, make it clear from the get-go what the expectations are for learners in your course so that they don't make any assumptions based on their prior experiences. In the absence of clear information from the designer, learners will simply use their prior learning experiences to inform how they behave in your course. As such, as a designer, make sure that the qualities that are unique in your course are clear. That way, learners know what to expect from your course and can be aware of the potential differences from any other learning experiences they've had. Do what you can, as the designer, to limit the potential for learners to make undue assumptions about the learning experience.

Navigating the Learning Environment

One of the biggest challenges for an online learner is understanding how to navigate the online course itself. Chances are, learners may be navigating whatever platform or learning management system you're designing in for potentially the first time. Even if learners in your course have had some prior experience with using the platform you're using, your approach as a designer may be very different from the approaches of other designers. Therefore, establish clear expectations for the following:

- How to navigate the course website or learning management system.
- What to find in each section of the course website or learning management system.
- How often you expect learners to engage with certain tools or features in the course platform or learning management system.

To establish these expectations, create an orientation video to demonstrate what it looks like to navigate through the course site. Anticipate what questions your learners might have about certain navigational sections of your course website in the orientation video and address those accordingly. Then take a screenshot image of the course website and annotate the image with your comments or guidance on what each button is for on the course website. That will provide an alternative to watching a full video for learners who just want a quick orientation to what the course website looks like.

Whenever you create multimedia resources, be sure that you're simultaneously creating simple text transcripts and versions of your documents so that they are accessible to all learners. For example, a simple text document explanation of what each major section of the course website includes would be an accessible version of an annotated screenshot (see Figure 3.3).

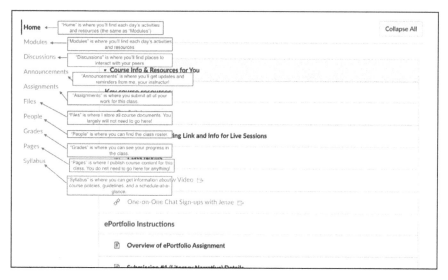

FIGURE 3.3
An annotated version of the course website orients learners to what they can find on each section so that they know what to expect when they click on each page.

NOTE AVOID TOO MANY CLICKS TO FIND CORE CONTENT

As a designer, you may have limited control over the organization and navigation of learning content in the website or learning management system that you're using. However, helping learners navigate through their experience with the fewest number of clicks or movements back to a landing page is better.

Devin Chaloux, the Director of Learner Success at Esme Learning, suggests making a learning experience feel as seamless as reading a book from front-to-back: make sure that activities are sequenced in an order that's as intuitive as possible. Chaloux says, "The more tasks that you ask someone to do, the more that you introduce disruption." Tools alone will not mitigate this potential for disruption, however. Try thinking intentionally about the most common sequences through the courses that learners are likely to follow.

Communicating What's in It for the Learner

From the start, learners will want to understand what they will get out of the course. In order to stick with the learning experience and not give up right away, they will want to have a very clear understanding of what they should be able to do, learn, or understand when the course is completed.

As such, one of the first pieces of content in your course should be a statement of what are often called *course learning outcomes*. We discussed writing learning goals earlier in this chapter already, but there's a difference between *writing* outcomes for your design process and *communicating* these outcomes to your learners. Sometimes, course outcomes can feel inauthentic or abstract for learners, even if they're helpful to you as the designer. To avoid this problem when writing outcomes directed toward your learners, be sure to:

- Use action-oriented verbs, such as "apply," "investigate," "develop," "write," "interpret," etc.
- Keep your outcome statements limited to a one-sentence maximum.
- Try pairing your outcome statement with an icon or illustration.

Ask colleagues, friends, and family to read your outcomes, too. When you aim to write outcomes in plain, nontechnical language, you will make the goals even clearer for the learners you're reaching.

Using the learning goals for the meditation class again, here are a few examples of effective outcome statements:

- Use breathing to relieve stress.
- Apply mindfulness techniques in your daily lives.
- Create a weekly meditation plan to keep yourself on track with your goals that you can use both in the class and beyond it.

Keeping Track of Success

As a learner-centered designer, your goal is to make the pathway to learner success as smooth as possible. Bad learning design should not be a barrier to completion.

The most important thing that learners will probably want to know from the start is about how to pass or complete the course. Whether "success" in the course means accessing a set number of materials, passing a series of quizzes, or submitting a project or written assignment, learners will want to know right away what they need to do in order to earn the appropriate credit or proof of completion.

Set clear expectations up front about how learners will know that they're succeeding in the course. Will all of the feedback be automated? Will some of the feedback be from the facilitator? From peers? Helping learners understand how they can check in on their understanding will make learners feel that their primary concern—being successful in the course—has been heard. We'll talk more about some of these options for assessing learners' understanding of the content in Chapter 10, "Giving Your Learners Feedback."

Completion through a course should be visible and obvious. Many modern eLearning authoring software solutions include clear indicators of progress. For example, Adobe Captivate includes a progress bar that shows what percentage of a course is completed (see Figure 3.4). Even if the authoring software or learning management system that you're using does not include that progress bar, giving a clear indication through the use of a Table of Contents or simply the use of a visual symbol to indicate progress completion helps learners stay oriented to where they are in the experience.

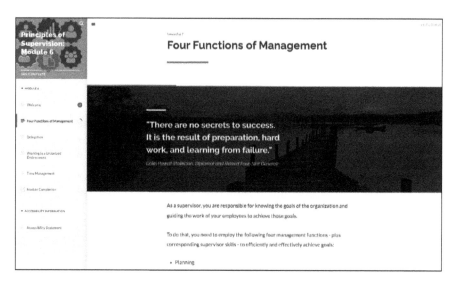

FIGURE 3.4

The use of design choices helps learners keep track of progress throughout the course, including the completion bar in the upper-left corner and a symbol next to each section in the learning units that shows how much of the section has been completed.

If your course requires learners to submit work or complete any kind of evaluations, like quizzes, designing your course in a way that allows learners to see evidence of task and assignment completion alongside course content completion will help learners keep track of their success. Even if automated assessments are used, knowing which assessments learners "passed" or "failed" will help learners understand their progress not just toward completion, but understanding.

Giving your learners this orientation to where they're going in the course—and helping them remember where they've been—sets the foundation for a learning experience that offers transparent expectations all the way through.

Takeaways

- **Start at the end.** Having a clear sense of the end goal for the course is the single greatest thing you can do to design a successful learning experience.

- **Identify the problem you are solving for learners.** The more you know about your learners, the more confident you are likely to feel about your ability to identify and define their problems and needs.

- **Define an endpoint.** An endpoint statement is a representation of your learners when they reach the end of your course or learning experience.

- **Create learning goals.** Present a short list of things that learners need to know and be able to do by the end of the learning experience.

- **Build a learning map.** A learning map connects the main problem or problems to be solved, the learner endpoint, and a list of learning goals.

Building a Space for Online Learning

Constructing an online learning space is a challenge because the space where learning is happening—the internet—is not a space exclusively designed for learning. A laptop, a smartphone, or a tablet can become a place where learners may join an online class, and yet they do all kinds of things from these devices besides learning. They pay bills, read the news, watch movies, chat with friends, shop for clothing, and almost anything else that may be completely unrelated to a learning experience.

In a physical, on-site classroom, there are chairs and tables and other sets of defined spaces where the roles for the learners and the instructor are tacitly clear. But online learning is not really "a space" at all. Virtual learning can happen anywhere, which sometimes means that it can feel like nowhere. That means online learners often start out feeling disoriented. Once they log in—which may be a challenging process in and of itself—then what? There may be a link or some kind of menu or table of contents, but it is often unclear where to go and what to do after finding that link.

Without the familiar signposts that define an on-site classroom, an online learning experience often begins with a search for anything that looks like the place for where to go next. The learning experience begins with a feeling of being lost or disoriented—hardly the best way to begin.

If you are relatively new to online instruction, you may be tempted to model your course designs on the familiar model of on-site learning. Re-creating on-site learning often means that the designer falls back on a heavy use of recorded lectures in the form of videos that can be long—often an hour or even longer. Trying to re-create an on-site space online is not only unimaginative, but often unsuccessful. These approaches reproduce assumptions about what learning *should* look like: passive and instructor centered. However, learners don't want to sit and passively watch lectures all the time, whether they are recorded or live.

The online learning space offers unique opportunities to reimagine what learning can be because it is fundamentally different from an on-site space. That means online learning designers have an opportunity to prioritize the online learner's experience in contrast to passive, instructor-centered models. By exploring the distinct principles and practices that guide what's possible in an online space, designers can align the best of the online medium with the opportunity to re-center learners and their experiences.

What's Different About Online Learning

As an online learning designer, think of yourself as an architect: You have the tools to build the floor plan, layout, and flow of a brand-new learning space. You don't have to work just with "the bones" of an existing building; rather, you get to create an entirely new learning blueprint. Too many learning designers think of themselves as interior decorators who simply try to "spruce up" an existing learning space, but who keep the same fundamental principles of an on-site learning experience at the core of the design process.

Rather than trying to wedge online learning principles into a space built for on-site engagements, shift your orientation as a learning designer to re-create what's possible in a class space. It will make a world of difference in terms of your learning experience's outcomes and potential for learner engagement.

Embrace Learners' Agency

It is impossible to control where and how users access a website. That's a good thing. In fact, a lot of user experience researchers relish understanding the multiple pathways that a user can take to complete a task. Yet, still other online learning designers want to lock down the learner agency in a course. For example, learning management systems and training websites often offer designers the option to keep certain pieces of content inaccessible until a user has completed prior work in the course. Other options for controlling learner agency include "timing out" access to particular pieces of content or preventing users from opening additional windows in a browser or on a computer so that the learner is not "distracted" from engaging with the course material on the course website.

These kinds of practices aim to control the learner's experience. In some cases, there may be value in trying to help steer learners in just one direction. Some content may require deep practice and knowledge with one concept before learners can move on to another. However, locking down access to parts of a course communicates that the designer is assuming the worst of learners—that they will be distracted while learning online. This lack of trust is transparent and will likely have the effect of making students feel frustrated and annoyed, mindsets that are not conducive to being engaged in a learning experience. If you design one linear learning path, you put the learners "on rails" and guide them directly to a single goal. Usually, you want to offer two or three options for each topic or lesson.

Creating additional options may mean more work for you as the learning designer (see Figure 4.1). But this extra work is well worth it to create additional trust, buy-in, and freedom for your students in ways that are well-aligned with the online learning environment. For example, if an activity requires that a learner watch a video, consider also giving the learner an option to read a transcript of the video or listen instead to a podcast that covers the same concepts. These extra options will require only a minimal amount of design time and will give the student significant flexibility in terms of how they'd prefer to engage with the content.

Another example of creating an additional learning option might be in how the student demonstrates evidence of their learning. Instead of writing a response to a question, a learner could record a voice memo detailing their response or create a mind map or visual instead of a written answer.

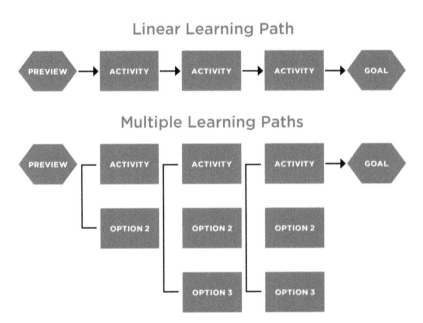

FIGURE 4.1

There are two ways a course can be designed for a learner: by following a linear path where a learner sequentially moves through a tracked set of activities or by having a choice of multiple learning paths where several activity options are available to reach the same goal.

Some educators worry that by creating multiple learning paths, they may not be able to fairly assess all learners' engagement in the same way. It may, for example, be too challenging to tell whether a learner really "got it" if they record a voice memo response rather than writing a text-based answer. As a learning designer, think back to the learning goals of the course: Can you look at the product the learner created and see how they are achieving the outcomes of the course? There may be cases where the product of the work itself needs to be rigidly defined. But there are many cases where the end product may not matter as much as the process the learner went through in order to create the end product. Hone in on what you really want the learner to know. Then, you may be surprised to discover that there is more than one way to demonstrate evidence of learning.

Learners not only appreciate having some freedom and agency in deciding where, how, and when they access particular parts of a course, but for some learners, this freedom may be essential to their success. Preventing learners from opening up another browser window while accessing content in the course may prevent someone for whom English is not their first language from accessing an online dictionary or translation tool to understand a core concept. Locking access to future content in a course may prevent a learner with ADHD from being able to flip back and forth between concepts and plan for how they might manage their time in the course.

Remember that if you have already created a learning map (see Chapter 3, "Setting the Foundation"), you can review your map and use it to revisit your learning goals in order to create flexible pathways for learner choices. Your learning map should reorient you to the problem or problems you are trying to solve with your design, the endpoint you want your students to arrive at, and your main goals for the learners, even as you're creating options and flexibility.

While designers can't anticipate every possible learner and situation, they should aim to design their courses in ways that communicate their trust in the learner. Any design decisions that constrain learner choices indicate a lack of trust that their learners will make choices that are meaningful to them. Creating, rather than closing down, options will likely help more learners feel like they can access, engage, and appreciate the course content.

Some learning designers may be asked to update courses that have already been designed by someone else. In this situation, a learning designer is less of an architect and more of a builder for a set of new tract homes in a preplanned development. Updating or building within a predesigned course does not have to be completely constraining, and many core online learning design principles can be put into practice.

If you are working with a predesigned course created by someone else, build in opportunities for student engagement whenever possible. Predesigned courses tend to streamline how the course content is presented. However, there is typically room for customization around learner interactions and instructor preferences. You should aim to generate activities that will bring out student personalities and interests, even if the content itself is streamlined in a standardized way.

Try to create media to increase learner engagement. Many predesigned courses are mostly text-based with short quizzes at the end of each unit. Creating even a few multimedia pieces, like short videos to explain key ideas, or to introduce projects or activities, can have a big effect on learners' ability to complete units more effectively.

Finally, check for out-of-date references or details that may make the course appear to be created in cookie-cutter fashion. Learners will see that an online course is a copy of another course if there are references or materials that appear obviously dated. Work to eliminate these references while incorporating some specific or personal details that may be relevant to the group of learners that you're designing for so that the material feels custom-made even if it is part of a standard sequence.

Zoom Is Not Your Classroom

Learning designers are fortunate to have many tools at their disposal for facilitating real-time interactions online. Video conferencing is an easy way to connect and have live conversations. However, over-reliance on video conferencing can be a problem.

Real-time interaction requires a lot of time, energy, and attention. When a learner joins a video conference, they are prepared to pay attention, talk to others, take notes, ask questions, and be present. Managing all of these tasks may not seem like a big deal, especially if these kinds of tasks are expected for an on-site instead of an online learning experience. However, engaging in all of these activities online can often feel more effortful than doing the same activities in an on-site space because the learner is responsible for creating an adequate environment to pay attention in. When you structure a video call like you would a live, on-site class session, you're assuming that the learner has a space that's quiet, spacious, and free of distractions. While some learners may be prepared for that situation, others may not be.

In fact, as learning designers, we've encountered one question time and time again about video conferencing: *Should video call participants be required to have their cameras on?*

This is a well-intentioned question because it suggests to us that learning facilitators would like to see the facial expressions and reactions of learners on their calls. Reading facial expressions and body language can be an important way to gauge interest, engagement, and focus. But just because someone *looks* engaged doesn't mean they *are* actually engaged. And many folks who don't look engaged on-camera could very well be intensely focused. If you're relying upon the visual cues of your participants to tell if they're actively engaged in the call, you're relying upon a pretty narrow band of information.

When you judge participation based on how someone looks or acts on the call, you may be lured into acting upon implicit biases that you may have about the people on your calls. To put it more bluntly, judging participation and engagement based on whether participants are smiling, nodding, or looking "focused" may reinforce a whole set of biases that could be ableist, ageist, sexist, and racist. Think about the pressures on women to "smile" in professional settings, for example (otherwise, they may seem "mean" or "angry"). Or think about the pressures on people of color to appear "amiable" so that they don't seem "intimidating." As a facilitator, it might feel good for you to see faces, but for your participants, putting on appearances in front of the camera could cause a bundle of worries that might distract them from the learning experience.

We know it feels strange to talk to a bunch of blank squares or still image avatars. However, if you design a real-time online learning experience with varied activities, multiple ways to participate, and a variety of options to get learners actively involved in the conversation, you shouldn't need to worry about having the camera turned on at all. You'll be able to understand whether learners are present simply by their engagement in the activities you've designed to capitalize upon the precious value of shared time together.

"Zoom fatigue" is real. Staring at a screen and a camera at other people for hours on end is not the same thing as entering into an on-site space where other people are gathered. A learner's body is much more constrained staring at the screen than they might be if they were sitting at a desk or in a conference room.

If an entire class experience is designed to take place in real time over video, it limits the chances for learners to process information at their own pace and on their own time. That doesn't mean that the learning experience can't include some real-time video conferencing components. On the contrary, learning designers will likely want to consider the benefits of real-time interactions for interactive components to the experience, like small group conversations, one-on-one talks, or activities like creating group whiteboards or collaborative notes.

But most learners will process material at different paces and may need options for engaging with course content beyond listening in real time or trying to absorb all of the concepts needed within only one time window. Given how demanding it is to video conference, save the live moments for activities where interaction is truly necessary and instead consider how other online tools can facilitate learning in a greater diversity of ways. That might mean using more prerecorded video to capture core ideas for the course. Other times, it might mean going even "lower-tech" by asking learners to read an article or contribute to a discussion board (or through a text-based chat tool, like Slack or Microsoft Teams).

Relying on video conferencing means putting a lot of work on your learners to process a lot of information all bunched together in real time. If you really want to take advantage of the true benefits of real-time dialogue with participants, you have to be intentional about how you align the modality of a live call with the media that you'll use in that call to engage learners in various activities.

Be Intentional: Align Activity, Purpose, Media, Modality

In any learning environment, you have to be intentional about how the space you use aligns with the activity you're facilitating. For example, you wouldn't ask someone to draw a picture if they didn't have a pen or marker available to use. The same principle applies in an online setting: You wouldn't ask someone to do something without the essential materials or environment.

Think first about the kinds of engagements you want learners to have. Then consider how those types of engagements can be facilitated within the online medium. That approach might mean using a video conferencing tool like Zoom, but it also might mean taking advantage of other tools and environments that may be available to learners in your course. And if you are going to use a video conferencing tool, you'll also want to consider what's available within that tool and how learners can really take advantage of what makes that environment unique.

Here's an example: Let's say that you want learners in your class to watch a video clip together in real time and then discuss the video clip. You could ask the learners to watch the video prior to coming to the real-time online session. However, what if there is content in the video that you want leaners in your class to respond to with their immediate reactions? You'll want to think about ways to take full advantage of the shared experience. For example, you could stream the video and have participants share their reactions by raising their hands and "unmuting" a microphone. You could also ask participants to type into the chat a response to a particular written prompt. Or you might administer a poll where the learners could perform a real-time "temperature" check on their response to the video.

In this case, creating a shared experience not only will happen in terms of watching the video itself, but will also be facilitated by online-centric activities—having learners share their reactions, asking learners to write their immediate responses in a chat space, or responding to the live poll. The learners will get to interact nimbly and in ways that make sense for the online environment.

Try putting an activity-first mindset into practice by listing all the possible activities that may be facilitated in your course. You could do that in the form of a table (see Table 4.1). After listing the activities in one column, put an explanation of the purpose of those activities in the next column. Why are these activities important in your particular class context? From there, look at the activity idea, then the purpose, and then start to brainstorm all the possible ways the activity could be accomplished online. What could learners do to engage in that activity? From there, you could start to brainstorm the tools and environments that you have available to you online to engage in that activity successfully.

TABLE 4.1 ONLINE APPROACHES AND TOOLS FOR FACILITATING
LEARNING ACTIVITIES

Learning Activity	Purpose
Define a key term and apply it to a professional situation	To understand how a key term and process can inform a professional situation
Small group discussion	To encourage learners to hear multiple perspectives on a key topic in the course
Large group discussion	To give everyone in the learning experience a sense of what the rest of the group thinks about a particular idea or concept

Possible Online Approaches	Tools Needed
Watch a video and take a quiz. Respond to a role-play scenario in a discussion board.	Video streaming platform (e.g., YouTube) Quizzing tool (e.g., Quizlet) Discussion board tool (e.g., in a learning management system, in Google Groups, or in Microsoft Teams)
Host a video conference call where learners could be broken up into small breakout rooms with discussion question prompts. Schedule a live chat where learners send text messages to each other in response to prompts in real time.	Video conferencing tool (e.g., Zoom) Chat tool (e.g., Slack, Microsoft Teams)
Host a video conference call where learners take a live poll together. The facilitator then asks members of the large group to answer some follow-up questions on the poll results in the chat or solicits feedback from individual participants willing to raise their hand and come on the microphone. Create a discussion board post question where members of the class are invited to respond. Make the question clear and specific so that everyone has an equal understanding about how to respond to the question.	Video conferencing tool (e.g., Zoom) Live polling tool (e.g., Poll Everywhere, Mentimeter) Discussion forum tool (e.g., in a learning management system, in Google Groups, or in Microsoft Teams)

Don't work against built-in features for online tools. For example, chat is a primary feature of a lot of video conferencing tools, but many learning designers are concerned that the usage of the chat feature can be distracting from what's being spoken during the video event. However, locking down this feature prevents learners and instructors alike from interacting with each other outside of speaking on the call. A facilitator can be more intentional about the use of the chat feature by explaining that the chat feature can be used to ask questions, respond to questions, or even just comment on what they're learning in the class.

CONSIDERING IMMERSIVE TECHNOLOGIES

Choices for which tools or modalities to use to engage with learners could become even more complex by the increasingly widespread availability of immersive technologies, such as virtual reality (VR), augmented reality (AR), and extended reality (XR). These kinds of immersive technologies are also sometimes referred to as *the metaverse*. Not all learners can engage with immersive technology equally because of the expensive costs, the restrictions and challenges in using VR equipment, and limitations in accessing affordable educational programs or software. However, many colleges, universities, and training programs are considering the options available with VR, and it may be worth thinking about its functionality, depending on the content of the course you're designing and the audiences for whom you may be designing.

Renata Mares, a nurse-educator who teaches at McMaster University and who designs eLearning experiences for nurses, has identified several benefits for using VR in medical education contexts. Mares says that "VR is a safe place to practice very dangerous activities. Let's say you're a first-year nursing student and, in the practice VR experience, you accidentally overdose a client. It's OK to do that, and you learn the steps to never do it again. VR is not a magic bullet; you still need the hospital setting. But it gives learners a bird's-eye view so that you can practice longer and not burn out from your profession."

Maximize Your Design for Engagement

Jenae once had an experience of taking a course on inclusive hiring practices online. This course was designed to help her learn some effective practices when serving on job search committees to ensure fair and equal treatment of candidates within a hiring pool. The course contained several quizzes throughout, but Jenae quickly discovered that the quiz questions were basically just reiterated versions of sentences she had encountered in the course. While the course was estimated to take an hour, Jenae completed it in 15 minutes because she could use the "find" and "search" tool on her keyboard to find the exact phrases and hunt for the answers to the quiz.

This process wasn't a very effective way to learn. And while the quiz had some interactive content, it wasn't a very creative way to approach the process, nor did it consider how participants could simply look up the answers (like Jenae did).

A better approach would have been to design quiz questions for the inclusive hiring course that were situational. Perhaps the course could have displayed an imaginary résumé for a potential job candidate and asked quiz takers to respond to a multiple-choice quiz with possible ways to react or respond to the résumé. Better yet, perhaps the quiz question could have included some drag-and-drop menus where learners could drag filled-in responses of how they might use or consider information from different parts of the résumé in their own assessment of the candidate based on a job ad.

In short, if the designers had thought carefully about the full extent of activities and learning experiences possible online, the learners could have had a much more substantive and positive experience in the course.

Any one tool alone, including a video conferencing tool, is going to be a poor replacement for any kind of on-site learning space. Being online means taking advantage of a whole cluster of tools to ensure that the space is aligned well with the experience.

Takeaways

- **Think like an architect.** Rethink your course designs and develop modular activities that guide learners on a clear learning path.
- **Design for trust.** Give learners multiple ways to complete an activity or lesson.
- **Chunk content.** Break things into smaller units for learners on mobile devices.
- **Limit your use of live video.** Video demands attention and time for you and your learners.
- **Use the right tool for the purpose.** Align your purpose with the activity and media for each activity.
- **Use multimedia to engage learners.** People learn better from words and pictures than from words alone.

CHAPTER 5

Designing Texts

Text forms the backbone of the online learning experience. Words are the connection to your learners—sometimes the only connection. Some learning experiences are composed entirely of words; others mix in media and visual content. No matter what the balance of text and multimedia in your online learning experience, the quality of the overall learning experience depends on your ability to compose texts that are clear, understandable, and usable.

You might like to think that every person reads the content that you write for an online course with focused attention and care. The reality is that readers will often be distracted, stressed, or mentally overloaded. Learners will not hang on to your every word. However, you can make your words easier to find, understand, and act on.

Think of a learner logging in to one of your courses. It's 10 p.m., and she's just now sitting down to start working on a lesson. The kids are finally asleep, and she has an hour to focus on the material. Your goal as a learning designer is to remove as many obstacles in her path as you can. You certainly don't want unclear language or confusing instructions to slow her down or make her learning any harder than it already is.

The texts that make up an online learning experience need to be written clearly, but they also need to be designed. Designing texts includes the arrangement of text on the page and other visual elements, in addition to writing the words and sentences. Even white space—the space between the words—is an important part of making texts readable and usable. As UX writers Michael J. Metts and Andy Welfle explain, "Writing is about fitting words together; designing is solving problems for your users."[1] Learning designers are often doing both at the same time.

You are using words to solve problems for your learners. Words do a lot of work to orient learners, help them find things, gain new knowledge, and build confidence in their learning. In Chapters 6, "Planning Videos," and 7, "Producing Videos," we'll look at interactive texts and media, including audio and video, but setting the foundation of usable, accessible text is a valuable first step for creating an effectively designed learning experience. Well-designed texts

---

1   Michael J. Metts and Andy Welfle, *Writing Is Designing: Words and the User Experience* (New York: Rosenfeld Media, 2020).

create an experience that helps learners feel more confident and able to understand the content they need to learn.

NOTE UX WRITING

UX writing is a growing subfield of user experience design. UX writers compose texts like menus, buttons, and labels that enable users to navigate through a digital product or website. Some of this written content, like menus and error messages, is called *microcopy*. UX writers work to ensure that any text that appears in a digital product is aligned with the values and ethics of their particular organization and is usable and accessible for all users.

Instructional Text

Instructional text is the connective tissue that binds together an online course. Clear instructional text engages learners and guides them toward goals and actions. Menus and links are part of the text in an online learning experience, but the instructional text does the work of the actual teaching. Think about a traditional on-site class. In that setting, the instructor will give lectures or explain ideas by speaking. In the online setting, all of that instruction happens in the writing.

If you are teaching a traditional on-site class, you can circle back, answer questions, repeat things if your students are not following, and reiterate key ideas to make sure that they stick with your learners. In an online environment, you have to make sure that the words are clear enough to be understood and remembered by your learners. If you simply recorded your lectures, you would quickly find that you don't speak the same way you write. Speaking in a live classroom, you are probably much wordier and repetitious than you are on the page or screen. Your goal in writing instructional text is to be personal, organized, and concise.

In the sidebar, "An Example of Instructional Text," you can read an example of a typical piece of instructional text, drawn directly from one of Michael Metts's online courses. The style is informal, addressing the learners as "you." The purpose of this text is to introduce an assignment that the learners need to complete (Project 1.2). In order to keep the directions short, a longer Google Docs template is linked at the top of the page. (The students can download and print the project template if they choose, which most of them will do.) Even though this example comes from a graduate writing course, the language and tone are casual, as if the author is speaking directly to a student audience in person. As a learning designer, you need to think about how you present yourself as a teacher or guide on the screen in words. Writing instructional text like this takes some practice. In our own experience, we often edit and revise on-screen instructional text two or three times before posting it live.

AN EXAMPLE OF INSTRUCTIONAL TEXT

Project 1.2 will be your first opportunity to create some visual media. Its purpose is primarily to prompt you to think visually (as opposed to verbally) and to experiment with expressing yourself using nonverbal modes of communication.

Begin by thinking about your own writing process.

- Are you a linear writer, who starts with an outline and proceeds in an orderly fashion?
- Do you prefer to just start drafting and see where the words go?
- Are you a recursive reviser?
- What does your writing process look like?

Once you develop a sense of your own writing process as you see it now, create a visual representation of that process. Your goal is to describe your writing process to other students in the class—without using words!

You can choose to create any kind of visual you like. You could draw a sketch using pencil on paper (then take a photo and upload and share the photo). You could create a slide presentation, with each stage of your process on a new slide. You could create a photo montage (using a digital tool or paper cut-outs). You could create a flowchart, process map, or mind map. You could create a video. You can use any medium you like, as long as it is primarily visual, and can be posted and shared online for the rest of the class to view.

Start with Learner Intentions

What do your learners need to do with the text? Any piece of instructional text needs to have a clear purpose. Ask yourself if your learners will be able understand what they need to do after reading the text.

In the "Example Text from LX Pathways from iDesign" note, the overview text we cite comes from the free introductory section of a course designed by the instructional design company iDesign on common learning theories that instructional designers should understand. In this overview text, the writers set the context for why instructional designers should be aware of common learning theories and then orient the learners to what they can expect to find in the rest of the lesson about learning theories. The concept of "learning theories" may be new to learners and this example text does an effective job of quickly defining the unknown concept before using the rest of the (short) paragraph to let learners know what they can expect from the remainder of the lesson.

> **NOTE** EXAMPLE TEXT FROM LX PATHWAYS FROM iDESIGN
>
> "There are many different learning theories. In this module, you will learn about three of the most common theories: behaviorism, cognitivism, and constructivism. Each theory provides a unique view of learning and motivation. It is important to be able to identify which theory is utilized because each one has different implications for the selection of teaching strategies, regardless of whether you are in a traditional or virtual setting."[2]

Online learners are often goal oriented. They can be impatient with a lot of background information and often skip ahead to find out what they need to *do* next. You can support them by defining the purpose and intention of the text on the first section or page of your text.

---

2 "Common Learning Theories" in Instructional Designer Pathway course, iDesign, 2023, www.lxpathways.com/instructional-designer

Use Plain Language

Jargon and inflated language can be obstacles to learners, especially when those learners are speakers of different languages. In most situations, you should use plain language for instructional texts. Use the most common word rather than specialized terms, if possible. You may be surprised to learn that the U.S. government has actually defined what "plain language" means. Specifically, the Plain Writing Act of 2010 requires that U.S. federal agencies use language that the public can understand and use. The federal guidelines are designed to help writers write clear and plain language so that readers are able to do the following:

- Find what they need.
- Understand what they find.
- Use what they find to meet their needs.

These guidelines apply to writers working in federal agencies, but they are useful and applicable to any writing you may compose that is intended for a general, public audience.

Notice how the guidelines are focused on the learners, rather than the writer. Learners need to be able to find, understand, and use information that you have provided. Writing reader-centered prose often requires a shift in perspective. As a learning designer, your writing should be more like technical writing, which is audience focused and responsive to the context and needs of your audience.

NOTE COGNITIVE LOAD THEORY

Educational researchers have studied how the human mind processes information. One pillar of learning is that humans have a limited capacity to take in new information. So, one sure-fire way to overload learners' cognitive capacity is to use complex language and wordy sentences. If learners are already stressed or distracted, their capacity to take in new ideas is reduced. You don't want to add more mental load by using jargon and technical language. "Keep it simple" and "less is more" are fundamental principles of learning design that apply especially to the language you are using to convey new information to your learners.

Figure 5.1 is an image from the CDC, which shows how to use plain language to present medical information for a general audience. The main heading puts the main idea up front ("getting vaccinated can help protect children against COVID-19"). Notice, too, how the use of headings, bullet points, and bold type focuses the readers' attention. The gray box at the bottom of the screen provides links to other information for parents and caregivers. Overall, this is a well-designed piece of text that uses the plain language guidelines.

2. Getting vaccinated can help protect children against COVID-19.

Vaccinating children can:

- **Prevent children from getting seriously sick if they do get COVID-19.** COVID-19 vaccination continues to protect children against severe disease, including hospitalization. There is no way to tell in advance how children will be affected by COVID-19. Children with underlying medical conditions are more likely to get severely ill from COVID-19. However, healthy children without underlying medical conditions can also experience severe illness.

- **Give parents greater confidence for children to participate in childcare and school** and in sports, playdates, extracurricular activities, and other group activities.

 Tips for Parents and Caregivers:

- Learn more about protecting your family against COVID-19.
- Questions You Can Ask Your School to Learn More About Their COVID-19 Precautions

FIGURE 5.1

The CDC's website demonstrates how using plain language can make complex ideas generally actionable and easy for audiences to understand and use.

Chunk Content for Easy Access

You should think mobile first when it comes to designing text for your online learning experience. It's important to recognize that content designed for mobile devices can always stretch to fill larger viewports, like bigger monitors or laptops. The reverse is not always true. So, make sure that you test everything on a mobile device first in order to prioritize the relatively greater limitations of a mobile screen for reading and engaging with text.

Figure 5.2 is a screenshot with activity instructions from one of Michael's courses, formatted for desktop-sized monitors. It doesn't look too bad on a large screen. White spaces break up the text and bulleted lists help readability.

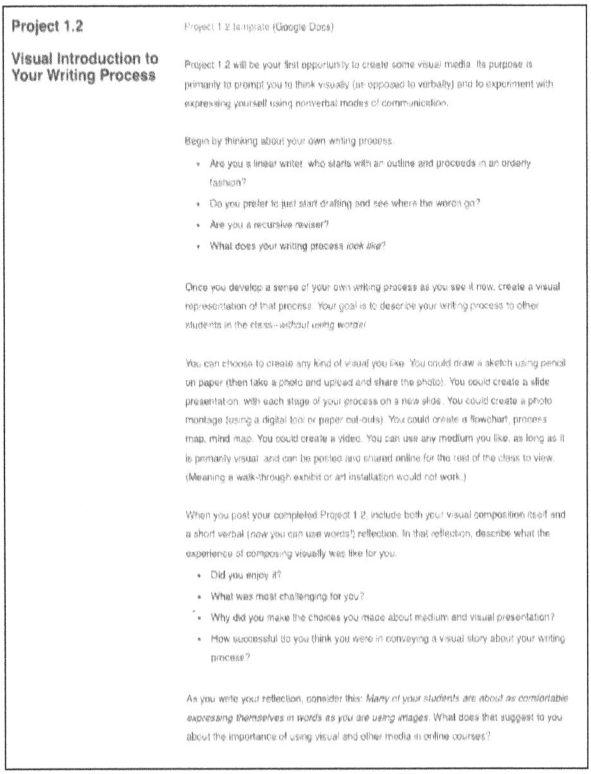

FIGURE 5.2

These instructions demonstrate a set of activity instructions that appear readable and well-spaced on a desktop display.

But on mobile? Suddenly that paragraph shown in Figure 5.3 looks pretty long. It would work better to edit the text and break that paragraph into two parts.

FIGURE 5.3

The same activity instructions from Figure 5.2 displayed on a mobile device appear too long and unwieldy when scaled for a mobile device.

Remember that your goal is to understand and experience your learning designs from a learner's viewpoint. While you might prefer to use a laptop with large monitors, that might not be how learners in your environment are working. Online learners are often working on mobile devices, and they can be prone to interruptions and distractions. If you design learning content around long texts designed for reading on long stretches of time, many of your learners will grow impatient. You may lose some of them.

Generally, the human mind can take in only about five to seven new items (words, images, or numbers) at a time. If you are stressed, that number goes down. Learning under stress quickly reduces your cognitive resources, which means that you might not even be able to take in five to seven new words alone. So, get really focused about what you want to include and think about the smallest units possible for communicating your ideas. For example, instead of one long text-based lesson, break the lesson into three or four short parts. Remember that you are designing for your learners, not for yourself.

Use Repetition to Create a Coherent Experience

Any important information in an online course should be in several places, because learners may not always find things in the first place they look. For example, learning designers know that placing important documents like a schedule or assignments in more than one place in a course website helps learners. Take advantage of the digital environment by using strategic repetition across your design from the organization of the site down to the sentence level.

Figure 5.4 uses repeated menu options; for example, the three sections of this course website are found in two places. Both the buttons across the bottom of the screen and the drop-down menu at the top lead to the same place: the three course outcomes of accessibility, presence and interaction, and course design.

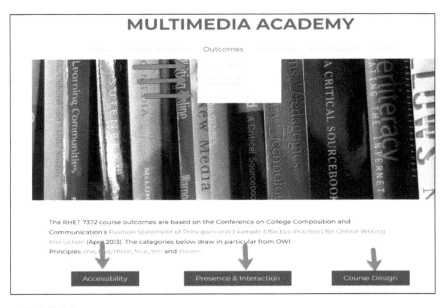

FIGURE 5.4

Michael's course website demonstrates the repetition of key terms and concepts in two places: in the drop-down menu and on the landing page of the course website.

You can also use repetition to link sentences together in a coherent chain. You may be tempted to use different words for the same idea to create a sense of variation, but you generally want to avoid that type of variation when you're writing instructions or activities. Learners can easily get confused if different words are used to mean the same thing. Your text may sound repetitious to you but remember that your learners are trying to understand a concept for the first time. Variation can create mental noise or confusion for them. Stick with one main word as you introduce a new concept or idea.

In this example from Codecademy, the word validation is the key idea being introduced. Yellow highlights are added to show how many times the repeated word is used to create coherence in the instructional text.

Introduction to HTML Form Validation[3]

Ever wonder how a login page actually works? Or why the combination of a username and password grants you access to a website? The answers lie in *validation*. Validation is the concept of checking user provided data against the required data.

There are different types of validation. One type is *server-side validation*, this happens when data is sent to another machine (typically a server) for validation. An example of this type of validation is the usage of a login page. The form on the login page accepts username and password input, then sends the data to a server that checks that the pair matches up correctly.

On the other hand, we use *client-side validation* if we want to check the data on the browser (the client). This validation occurs before data is sent to the server. Different browsers implement client-side validation differently, but it leads to the same outcome.

Arranging Information

Instructional texts are often directions that learners need to follow. To help learners, you want to organize information from the learner's point of view. If you want learners to follow a process step-by-step, organize the information in the same way. Don't jump around or backtrack or you risk losing your learners.

---

3   "Introduction to HTML Form Validation," Codecademy, accessed March 21, 2023, www.codecademy.com/courses/learn-html-forms/lessons/html-form-validation/exercises/validation-intro

Organize information from simple to complex. Think in terms of layers: Start with the main idea first and then add explanation or elaborate the first main idea. Start simple and then add details and complexity.

In the "Organizing Information in Context Example" sidebar (written for a graduate student audience), the first paragraph introduces the main project for the week ("create a writing assignment for students in your class"). The second paragraph expands to add details that are designed to explain the features of the assignment. Notice how each sentence in the second paragraph adds one new detail: the assignment should be "multimodal," "appropriate for students in the course you are teaching," "based in learning outcomes," and "student-facing." The third paragraph looks ahead to preview what the learners will be asked to do in the following week.

ORGANIZING INFORMATION IN CONTEXT EXAMPLE

Your primary goal for this week is to create a writing assignment for students in your class. This assignment will anchor the four-week learning unit you will develop in the course.

Your assignment should be multimodal, meaning that it prompts students to compose a text that includes images or media of some kind in addition to text. The assignment should be appropriate for students in the course you are teaching and should be based in learning outcomes specific to that course and student audience. The language of the assignment itself should be student-facing, meaning that it is written for readers at the level for which you are teaching.

In week three, a peer will role-play as a student in your class and write a composition in response to your assignment. For the purposes of this class, then, your assignment needs to be designed so that a peer could feasibly complete the assignment in one week.

Embrace Variety in Language and Design

Given that text is playing a lot of different roles in your online learning experiences—from activity instructions to content delivery and, perhaps in some cases, social interactions—think about how to design text in such a way that learners will recognize the variety of contexts in which they will be reading throughout the learning experience. It's easy to take the different roles that text and reading will play for granted in class. Instead, try to reduce the barriers to your learners' understanding of when and how they will use text in different ways in your class environment.

Consider, for example, using the same formatting for all assignment instructions so that learners have a very clear sense of when they're reading instructions rather than accessing content. Create a template for all assignment instructions. That way, components of the instructions, like the task of the assignment, are clearly labeled at the top of the page. Then the other components of the assignment (e.g., the purpose, the submission requirements, etc.) are all listed in the same order for each set of assignment instructions. That process will guarantee that a reader can quickly determine at-a-glance how they will engage with the text and the reading experience itself.

For text that's used for communicating content, ensure that there's a downloadable, offline version of the text that someone can read and access. It will signal to your learners that they may benefit from using tools outside of the course itself to engage with the reading, such as a PDF annotation tool or a text-to-speech tool.

Text will take on a lot of variety in your online courses; embrace the diversity of ways that you'll use language to guide and support learners throughout their experience.

Takeaways

- **Text is the foundation of an online learning experience.**
  Even if you've got a lot of other multimedia elements in your
  course, text will be a primary way that you communicate
  with learners and convey information.

- **Keep text plain and simple.** Avoid jargon and opt for common language that will be easily understandable by as many
  users as possible.

- **Don't write text, design it.** Think not just about what the
  words are in your course, but also how they appear and how
  their appearance will impact learners.

- **Test your text design on multiple kinds of devices.** Text
  will appear differently on a mobile device than on a desktop.
  You should design text that looks readable and accessible
  across multiple devices.

- **Intentionally repeat information in multiple ways.** Creating clear patterns for how information is conveyed will help
  key concepts stick and encourage goal-oriented behaviors in
  the learning experience.

CHAPTER 6

Planning Videos

Michael was teaching a new course and decided to produce a video for each week. In the early part of the course, he planned out each video and wrote individual scripts for each one. He kept the videos short—about five to seven minutes per video—and used the videos to explain a key concept from each week's course. As the term rolled along, Michael was pressed for time and started producing videos without scripting them first. Predictably, the videos got longer and longer. Some were almost 20 minutes long. Looking at the viewer stats, Michael began to notice a drop-off in views. By the end of the course, few students were even watching the videos at all. He was pretty depressed about this drop-off in student engagement around the videos.

Michael's story contains several important lessons for any learning designer who wants to create videos as part of their course content. First, keep the videos short! Michael discovered a sweet spot of around eight minutes. After that, learner engagement dropped off quickly. The second lesson was a little more subtle: course content, including videos, depends on context. At the beginning of a course, learners were eager, engaged, and soaked up new material. By the end, they were often tired and stressed, and wanted to focus on finishing their work (rather than watching the videos). What works in the second week of the course may not work in the tenth week. Planning and producing video content for online learners is highly dependent on the timing and overall rhythm of the course design.

For these reasons, learning designers need to create an overall plan for the learning experience itself before diving into the details of creating and producing media. (See Chapter 3, "Setting the Foundation," to learn about learning goals and how to design for time over a course experience.) It's easy to think that "every week needs a video," as Michael did. But the planning process needs to be more flexible and responsive to learner needs. Videos, more than any other medium, demand a higher degree of learner engagement and attention. Videos also demand a lot of time and effort on the designer's part as well.

Bottom line: Video can be a powerful and effective medium for instructional content but use it intentionally as part of the overall experience. Videos are best seen as punctuation in a learning experience rather than the experience itself.

Types of Instructional Video

To create a video that is intentional, engaging, and meaningful, you may want to learn something about the types of educational videos that other learning designers have made. That way, you can get a clearer sense of what's possible. Seeing good examples may also open up some new, creative ideas for your own video production. There are several genres of video to consider producing in the context of an online learning experience (see Table 6.1 on the next page).

Planning an Instructional Video

After you've identified the type of video you want to make, you get to dive into the fun part: mapping out your content and deciding what you want to include in your video. Identifying the type of video you want to make should have already helped you zoom in on its purpose. What do you want your video to accomplish? What do you want learners to get out of watching the video? The purpose and the conventions of the type of video you've chosen will remain at the core of the planning practices to come.

Storyboarding

Think about how you'd approach writing a report. Someone at some point probably suggested that you create an outline to help you map out your ideas well in advance of putting sentences together.

The same principle applies when you create a video: before you do any recording or producing, outline your video content. A good way to do that is in the form of a *storyboard*, which is a visual outline for your video. Because visuals are, arguably, the core and most important part of a video, a storyboard will allow you to outline simultaneously what you want viewers to see and hear as they watch the video. As the video designer, storyboarding will also enable you to plan ahead in terms of aligning the visuals you create with the script you'll use for the narrated content.

To start your storyboard, think of the scope of what you want to capture in your video. Remind yourself of your video's purpose and what you're hoping to accomplish. Then identify one small "chunk" of content you want to capture in five minutes or less. For example, what do you want your viewer to know by the time they finish watching the video? What's the one thing they should understand or be able to do by the time the video is complete?

TABLE 6.1 TYPES OF INSTRUCTIONAL VIDEOS

Types of Videos	Purpose	Examples
The Explainer	Explain a new concept, term, or idea.	"Does stress affect your memory?" (TED-Ed) "How Does Your Brain Learn?" (Alex Dainis via YouTube)
The How-To	Demonstrate how something works.	"How to Draw and Animate in PowerPoint with Inky Replay" (Echo Rivera via YouTube) "How to Use a Transfer Pipet" (Bio-Rad Explorer via YouTube)
The Story	Tell a story of someone else's experience.	"Example of Racial Discrimination in the Workplace" (Emtrain via YouTube) "Expanding a Cabin in the Arctic" (*National Geographic*)
The Personal Moment	Share a personal insight, experience, or a piece of advice.	"Creativity break: How can we combine ways of thinking in problem solving?" (Khan Academy) "A Day in the Life of a UX Writer" (Google Career Certificates via YouTube)

Watch Out!	What's Best
The explainer can easily become a boring "talking head" where a narrator simply gets on-camera and talks. Avoid creating "explainers" that simply replicate an in-person lecture experience.	Variety is key for this genre. Intersperse video of someone narrating the content alongside the use of other animations, illustrations, or live video footage to visualize what the narrator is explaining.
Too much detail will bog the viewer down. Try to think about what you can demonstrate in 5 minutes.	Create time-stamped markers in the video for each step in the process. That way, viewers can try the demonstration along with you and, if they need to take more time, they can easily pause and find their place again.
Storytelling should immerse your viewer in the experience. Even when there's something to learn from the story, try to keep any "explainers" or reflections on the significance of the story out of the video.	Create a character, establish a plot, and bring in a problem or a tension. These elements will keep your viewer interested in understanding what's going on.
Keep the scope limited here: This video is an opportunity to pull back the curtain and connect with learners emotionally. Don't get too much into course content here; that can be reserved for your explainers.	These videos are a great way to "humanize" an instructor or designer for the class. Simple is better for this one: film in a personal space that looks comfortable and homey.

After you've identified the scope of your content and what key points you want to make in your video, think about your visuals. Learners watching videos are going to notice what they see before they notice what they hear. And while you'll eventually need to sync the audio to the visuals, pinning down each visual or illustration for each concept in your video will make planning for the rest of your video much easier.

Once you're ready, start building your storyboard. Think in terms of 30-second intervals: What should your viewer see and hear in the first 30 seconds? The second 30 seconds?

You can do this by creating a quick sketch of what you'd like to see in each frame. Don't think too hard or spend too much time creating the perfect visuals yet. Rather, just try to map out what you'd like to have happen at each key moment in your video, as shown in Figure 6.1.

FIGURE 6.1
A simple nine-panel storyboard shows you the overall story arc and maps out key moments.[1]

You could also create a storyboard by using a slide tool, like PowerPoint or Google Slides. Use one slide to capture each main idea. Figures 6.2 and 6.3 offer examples of this practice. In these examples,

---

1   Donna Lichaw, *The User's Journey: Storymapping Products That People Love* (New York: Rosenfeld Media, 2016), 118.

Michael created slides for each section of a video he was creating to inform learners about how the publishing process worked. Each slide contained one step in the four-part publishing process: concept, development, design, and marketing. Using slides this way, as a type of storyboard, helped Michael organize and visualize how to present a complex process in visual form.

STORYBOARD PART ONE

STORYBOARD PART ONE

FIGURE 6.2

One way to create a storyboard is to create a series of slides in Keynote or PowerPoint, to map out the sequence of scenes for an instructional video. Here, Michael used Keynote to create a visual storyboard of a video for one of his classes.

FIGURE 6.3

Starting with static slides helps to imagine the visual content for each main idea or step in a process, as in this example of a storyboard created in the process of making a video about the publishing process.

Scripting

You may already have some sense of what you want to say at each point in your video when you've created your storyboard. However, your storyboard probably just includes some notes or bullet points of the text at each 30-second interval. Once you have a clear vision of your video's full arc, then you're ready to write the script where you can plan, word-for-word, what you want to say in the video.

Having a script written out will help you prioritize the most important content. It's easy to ramble on when improvising while you speak. If you have a script in front of you while you record, however, you'll be able to remember what you want to say more clearly and have your key points already prepared.

Reading off a script for a video will save you time in the long run when it comes to making sure that your video content is accessible, too. While a lot of video uploading and storage tools, like YouTube, have automatic captioning tools built in, the automatic captions are typically not entirely accurate. If you are relying on automatic captions, it's likely you'll need to edit the captions. To ensure greater accuracy, write your own script, and then upload your script along with your video to any storage platform you use.

As you write your script, practice reading your script out loud as you go. It might feel a little weird to talk to yourself while you're writing. However, when you're writing a script, you're writing words that are meant to be spoken, not read silently. Especially if you're new to writing scripts for video, you want to be sure that what you're writing on paper sounds good when it's read aloud, too.

When you read your script out loud to hear how it all sounds, put a stopwatch on at the same time. Different speakers will speak at different paces, so it will be helpful to learn roughly how many words you can write in your script to equate to a 2-, 3-, or 5-minute video. And while shorter chunks of content are, generally speaking, better for long-term retention and engagement, a 10-second video is not necessarily better than a 5-minute one. If your choice is between one 20-minute video, two 10-minute videos, four 5-minute videos, or ten 2-minute videos, think more holistically: what are the topics covered in the 20-minute version? The 10-minute version? From there, consider how the content can be divided in the clearest way possible with attention to how the chunked content might help a user understand one idea before moving on to the next one. Basically, if you find that your script is running long, consider where your video content might be chunked up.

Be sure to align what you're going to say alongside your visuals. It may be tempting to believe that you could improvise easily once you hit your "record" button and can see the visuals that you've prepared in front of you. However, once you press that "record" button, it's easy to forget what your intentions were when selecting particular visuals for your video. A script will help you remember why you thought certain visuals were important for the scope of the video you designed.

When your next step is to record, you're already accustomed to speaking the words. It's a guarantee that your speaking voice will sound a lot more natural (even when you're reading off a script!) if you've been practicing, revising, and hearing yourself all through the process.

Record yourself during your practice runs, too. It might be a little painful—hearing your own voice can feel a bit weird. But you have to hear how quickly (or slowly) you read, so that you have the opportunity to revise your script to either include more or less verbiage to align with your own speaking speed and style.

If you're creating a video for an audience of learners whom you think might not speak English as their first language, think about the cultural references you use and how quickly you speak. Imagine how you would feel if you were listening to a video in a second or third language: What would you need or appreciate from the narration that would help guarantee your understanding of the content?

Asking yourself these kinds of questions as you're preparing a video for different audiences will help you better align the choices you make in the script with the needs of your audience.

This is an example of a video script used for an online course developed by Jenae Cohn and Mary Stewart. This video was designed to give an overview of an assignment that college students in a first-year writing course had to complete. You'll notice that because this is a video intended largely for an audience of college students, the examples are geared toward background experiences that they would likely know or understand, like the SAT exam or going into a bookstore. The sentences are also short and sometimes incomplete because the script was designed with the intention of being spoken rather than read. Note that this is a script for a 3-minute video, and it's still quite long! So, bear in mind that even if the idea of creating a script for only three minutes of content sounds intimidatingly short, there's probably still quite a bit you can pack into a short period of time.

00:00–00:08

When you hear the word "genre," you might initially think of the signs you see when you walk into a bookstore—categories like "Science Fiction," "Mystery," "Romance."

00:08–00:23

When you hear the names of these literary genres, you probably have an image you associate with them. You might think of spaceships when you think of science fiction or a couple embracing when you think of romance. Literary genres help us to categorize and make sense of different trends in literature.

00:23–00:37

The word "genre" may also remind you of music or movies. Just like you might think of images of certain book covers when you hear the names of literary genres, you might think of certain sounds or lyrics when you hear the names of musical genres, like "pop," "country," or "hip-hop."

00:37–00:55

These concepts of genre help us to sort and classify artistic experiences. However, genres don't just help us categorize types of art. Genres can also have rhetorical power. They can evoke a certain set of cultural assumptions that are crucial to the art of persuasion and can help enact social change.

00:55–00:58

Let me give a really concrete example.

00:58–1:11

Imagine you're taking the SAT exam again. When you open up the SAT test, you probably have a very clear idea of what you expect to see: a booklet with a scantron and rows of multiple-choice questions.

1:11–1:29

What would happen if you opened the booklet and, instead, found hand-drawn pictures of zoo animals with large boxes for you to fill in with short answer responses? You would probably first think that you'd been given the wrong test. Why would a standardized test want you to respond to illustrations of zoo animals? What would be the purpose of that?

1:29–1:52

But someone else who had never seen a standardized test before might think the zoo animal exam was perfectly acceptable. The only reason you would know that that test is wrong somehow is because you'd been exposed to standardized tests before. You'd seen examples of what standardized tests looked like before you took the SAT. You would have a certain set of expectations about both the design and the content of the test.

1:52–2:14

You had been exposed to a genre: the standardized test genre. With that exposure, you likely came to understand two things: how a standardized test is designed and what it looks like to take a standardized test. That exposure to design and content helped you understand the purpose of the exam: to assess your learning. The design of the test informs the content of the exam.

2:14–2:26

It's important for you to know the definition of "genre" beyond the categories of shelves at the bookstore because understanding genre helps you to make choices about how you might appeal to different audiences.

2:26–2:39

Different audiences might have different expectations of genres, so it's important to consider the style, tone, and type of document you'd create and what that document might evoke for the audience member you're trying to communicate to.

2:39–2:48

The formal features of genres—what they look and sound like—are not arbitrary or meaningless.
Rather, the formal features of genres are connected to social purposes.

2:48–3:10

Experimenting with genre choices can actually be a lot of fun! Once you start looking for characteristics of different kinds of texts, videos, or audio files, you may find yourself appreciating those texts a lot more than you did before! In coming activities, you'll get a chance to research new genres on the web and decide which genre may be most appropriate for you to write in for your upcoming genre essay.

Creating Your Visuals

Before you record your video, you will need polished, shareable versions of your visuals. You'll have several factors to consider around decisions for your visuals, from how you'll create them to what effect you hope the visuals will have on your audience. Your visuals are going to be one of your most powerful tools in your videos, so take the time to think critically about what you're including.

As always, keep your audience top of mind. Different audiences will have differing reactions to your visuals, particularly if the visuals reflect a cultural reference or historical moment. For example, some learning designers may be drawn to using the image of a rocket ship to represent a "start" or "launch" point in a course. However, the rocket ship is not as universal of an image as it seems. The concept of space travel as representing a "beginning" or an "exploration" is deeply rooted in the American cultural imagery; it is not nearly as significant to learners from other countries where space travel is not as valued. As such, think through what kind of images or iconography may be truly universal and which may be more specific to the needs and understandings of your particular viewers.

Take Honest Inventory of Your Technical Skills

It's easy to get overwhelmed with the options for creating graphics online. Current graphic design tools, like Canva and Adobe Express, have drag-and-drop interfaces for editing photographs, creating icons, and designing beautiful images in ready-made designs. Drag-and-drop tools, however, may frustrate more advanced technical users; customization options are relatively limited within these tools and applying brand colors or logos may require premium accounts for usage. Keep these factors in mind as you decide what you want to use before you start building so that you don't have to cycle through too many different tools at once.

Keep Live Footage to a Minimum

For instructional video content, think very carefully about the value of any live footage you may need to capture. There may be contexts where you need to film yourself or another person doing something.

For example, if you're trying to film a process or a workflow that must be demonstrated with real-life objects, capturing live footage would make sense. And some learning designers may be in the fortunate position of partnering with a film production crew that could support your instructional vision. However, if you can portray a concept with an animation, a series of still graphics or photographs, or even just yourself speaking through a web camera, that will save you (and your client, company, or university) a lot of time and resources.

Filming live footage is tremendously difficult: capturing audio, lighting, and movement from live shoots requires technical skills that most learning designers will likely not have time to develop. More often than not, the concepts you're trying to capture can be portrayed just as easily with more abstract graphics or with cartoons that you can create through free and easy-to-use programs. If you are creating video footage on your own, you can probably create something that looks and sounds better from your own computer if you're not trying to use a lot of live footage.

Creating visuals for your video could take a lot or a little bit of time, depending on the goals for your video and how original you want the visuals to be. Having an abundance of visuals for a video is important, but if you are not a video producer, simple visuals, like icons, "b-roll footage," or stock video images can go a long way. Again, try to align what you're capable of making with what you want your video to look like and decide how you'll create your visual resources from there.

Elements of Visual Design

While you don't have to be a graphic designer to create good visuals for your video, it can be helpful to understand some basic principles of visual design so that you can make good choices when creating your visuals. Understanding the principles of visual design can also help you understand the impact that your visuals may have upon your viewer. Just as you'll be making deliberate choices about the language you're using in your course for your audience, you'll go through the same process of thinking about your visuals for your audience as well.

Line

Lines divide different sections of an image or document into multiple parts. Lines create order in something disorderly. A line can help viewers determine where to look or differentiate between different parts of an image.

For example, in the ending graphic from the video in Figure 6.4, the designer uses lines to separate the different components of the video for the viewer to follow up on. There are also lines separating how to access the UX certificate and subscribe to the Google HR channel's updates.

FIGURE 6.4

The video "A Day in the Life of a UX Writer," created by the YouTube channel, Google Career Certificates, demonstrates how the effective use of lines creates visual interest in the backdrop and shows how to access resources beyond the video itself.

Color

Color has a dual purpose: It can evoke emotions in the viewer while also helping the viewer distinguish between different pieces of information quickly. It is generally agreed upon that particular colors evoke different emotions than others: for example, colors like orange and red tend to convey warmth or passion, while colors like blue and purple tend to convey coolness or calm. But bear in mind these associations are culturally different, so consider where your audiences will be viewing your video from before making assumptions about the meanings of the colors for your viewers.

In the video shown in Figure 6.5, color is used to contrast the graphic image of the brain from the background. The use of the purple background and the green highlighted areas of the brain emphasize where the viewer should focus in order to understand the changes in active brain regions. It should be noted that this particular image is not going to be accessible for all viewers; for full color contrast, check all images with a color contrast verifier tool, such as the one available from WebAIM: https://webaim.org/resources/contrastchecker/.

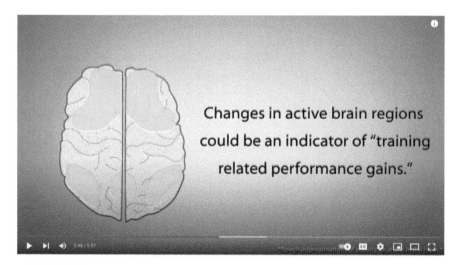

FIGURE 6.5
This video, "How Does Your Brain Learn?" by science communicator Alex Dainis, demonstrates how the use of bright pops of color distinguishes core pieces of content.

Shape

Most visual objects are derived from a few fundamental, basic shapes: circles, squares, and triangles. These shapes are useful for building abstractions of processes, like infographics and workflows.

In the TED-Ed video shown in Figure 6.6, "Is the weather actually becoming more extreme?" the artist renders different microclimates and ecosystems into individual square boxes. The use of different square shapes here demonstrates that even environments that are in very different places and that have different conditions may be treated equally or seen in the same way when understanding the scope and scale of climate change.

FIGURE 6.6
This TED-Ed video (written by R. Saravanan and directed by Hype CG) shows how different square shapes form a grid to demonstrate the variety of extreme weather patterns happening around the world.

Size

Some elements may be large while other elements are small. Typically, the elements that are larger sizes than other elements are of greater importance than the smaller elements. But larger things are not always more valuable; the other elements in the visual may visually draw attention to smaller-sized items so that you don't lose sight of the smaller parts of the visual entirely.

In the TED-Ed video, "Does stress affect your memory?" shown in Figure 6.7, the graphic artist uses an abstract representation of "information overload"—with a large pile of bags labeled "information"—to contrast with the smaller size of a desk labeled "Consolidation," meant to represent the human brain. The quantity of cartoon bags, labeled "information," reflects quickly and simply through size what it looks like when information overwhelms the other senses.

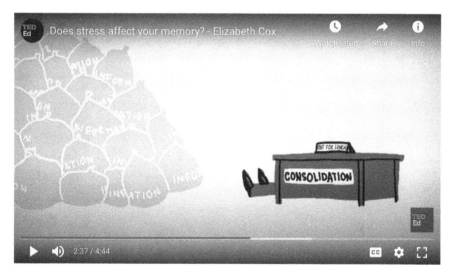

FIGURE 6.7

This TED-Ed video (written by Elizabeth Cox and directed by Artrake Studio) illustrates an abstract concept about cognitive load through extreme portrayals of size.

Space

Space is critical to help distinguish between the different elements in a visual. Without space, particular elements in the visual may be hard to distinguish or may have the effect that the visual is "busy" and, therefore, hard to read and understand.

In the Khan Academy video shown in Figure 6.8, "How can we combine ways of thinking in problem solving?" the text in the question-based prompts is surrounded by white space and abstract shapes in order to emphasize the text and draw attention to the core question that the video aims to answer.

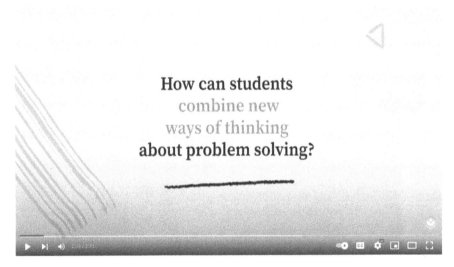

FIGURE 6.8
This Khan Academy video shows how the deliberate use of white space around the core question at the center of the screen makes the core question and idea stand out.

Value

Value refers to the lightness or darkness of a particular element in a visual. For example, think of a visual that may use different shades of the color blue; the elements that are darker blue than the lighter blue elements convey that the darker blue elements have greater value than the lighter blue elements. Just as something that is larger in size may signify greater importance than something that is smaller in size, something that is darker in color tends to signify greater value than something that is lighter in color.

Texture

Texture in an image may impact your orientation and understanding of what the image conveys. For example, a visual that includes lots of tiny dots may convey a bumpy texture, while a visual that includes lots of wavy lines and wavy images may convey a smoother or more "watery" texture. Texture might be used to evoke particular sensations in the viewer or distinguish between different elements in an image.

In AsapSCIENCE's video shown in Figure 6.9, "Is Calorie counting a scam?" they created a graphic to compare the ability to fully digest soy in North America and in Asia. The background of the image includes a textured pattern of soybeans. The textured background image emphasizes the content-based focus of the video (i.e., on food products) while demonstrating the soybean's prevalence around the world and in different kinds of diets. The use of texture makes the image more dynamic and reiterates the underlying importance of recognizing how dietary patterns around the world are connected to where food is grown.

FIGURE 6.9

The AsapSCIENCE video uses an image of soybeans as the background for a global map to create variety and texture in the background, while also illustrating the prevalence of soybeans around the world.

When using an image as a background to create texture, consider editing the background image to turn down the image's opacity from its raw form. This means going into an image editing tool and making the original image more transparent. That way, there is greater contrast between the background image and any potential foreground images or text. Reducing the opacity of the image will still generate the textured look and feel without distracting from the core information in the foreground.

Where to Create Visuals

After you've determined what kinds of visuals you want to create and what impacts you anticipate the visuals will have on your final product, think about the essentials: Where do you want to actually make your visuals?

Learning designers have some options for creating simple visuals, even without using formal or technical graphic design tools. If you have a graphic design background or have learned to use industry-standard graphic design tools, like Adobe Photoshop or Illustrator, then you have something of a head start and can create high-quality, customized graphics. However, if you don't have this background or the skills to engage with highly technical tools, there are plenty of other options.

To make simple graphics, use slideware tools, like Microsoft PowerPoint or Google Slides. Most slideware tools allow users to create simple shapes, graphics, and diagrams on the slides themselves. The slides can then be exported into graphical image files (for example, JPG or PNG files), which can be used in more customizable ways as needed.

If you want to create more complex visuals, try to use "freemium" image creation tools, like Canva or Adobe Express, to modify templates made by experts. If you're reluctant to make an image or a graphic entirely from scratch, image creation software like Canva and Adobe Express enable you to start from templates and then modify the templates to meet your needs. Many of these tools are "freemium" and may restrict some features without a paid license.

FINDING IMAGES AND PHOTOS WITH COPYRIGHT LAW IN MIND

When you're finding visuals for your video, whether they are photographs, icons, or cartoons, look for images that are either Creative Commons-licensed or are stock images or photographs. Any image explicitly licensed for free use can be used for a learning design video. Many free stock image libraries allow users to search by keywords to find images, from photographs to illustrations, that may meet their needs, like Pexels, Pixabay, and Creative Commons.

If you choose to use a search engine to find your images, bear in mind that you will need to go in and set your advanced search setting filters to identify only images that can be freely licensed and reused. Assume that most photographs available on the internet are copyrighted and cannot be used without paying royalties to the creator. Your best and easiest bet for avoiding a copyright battle is to search by default for images and photographs that the creator has already granted permission to use. It is a good practice to offer credit for any images used, however, and if you are producing a course that will generate revenue, it is a best practice to reach out to the image creator, request permission, and offer a stipend to use the image.

If all else fails and if you are really struggling to create or find the right graphics that you need for your video, you can rely upon using footage of yourself as the narrator speaking to generate a visual for your video. Seeing a human face, even for a brief period of time, can help with making the content feel like it's coming from a real person. But use your own image sparingly; watching a video that's just someone talking without any other visual elements will likely be boring for the viewer to watch for a sustained amount of time.

There is a substantial amount of planning that goes into creating a video. Taking the necessary steps to conceptualize and design a video will make the production process easier and faster to tackle next.

Takeaways

- **Keep video content short.** It's better to create several shorter videos than a smaller number of long videos.

- **Identify the type of video you want to create.** Not all instructional videos are the same. Learn from examples, know what your goals are, and plan from there.

- **Plan ahead.** Create a storyboard and a script to map out what you want viewers to see and hear as they watch your video.

- **Practice narrating your video.** Practice how you will sound and what you will say—it will go a long way toward making a higher-quality video.

- **Be aware of licensing restrictions and copyright concerns when selecting images or music for your video.** Assume that any images or music you find online for free are copyrighted unless they are explicitly noted by the creator as freely available to use and reuse (often with appropriate attribution).

Producing Videos

P roducing an instructional video brings together two sets of skills: technology skills to make the software work the way you want it to and design skills to ensure that your final product flows smoothly to achieve your instructional goals. Video production is something that many learning designers fear the most. That fear is understandable because producing a video is technically and mentally demanding. But when you pull together all the pieces and produce your video, you will feel a real sense of accomplishment. A good instructional video connects deeply with learners and helps them retain new information better than any other medium. It's hard work, but it's worth it.

Rest assured that you do not need to have been trained in professional video editing techniques to produce a quality instructional video. Obviously, the work of a professional video producer will elevate the technical quality of the video itself, and some learning designers may even partner with a professional producer to finalize their content. But generally, knowing some tips for what producing a final video can look like will help increase your capacity to use video thoughtfully throughout your learning experience.

Production Process and Workflow

There is certainly no one best way to produce a video, but you do need a process of some kind. This process should be simple and repeatable. Having a repeatable workflow process will help you focus on the content of the video rather than the technical details of the software. Like any complex process, producing videos will reward practice and repetition.

To illustrate the potential variation in the video production process, we will summarize our own processes, since we've developed them through a lot of practice.

Jenae's Process

I like to start by writing my script first. I think in terms of words and what I want to say in the video. What's the main message I want to deliver? After I've written that out, I take each of the segments of the script and create a table where I find an image (or two) that I think matches each component of the script. That forms my very basic storyboard concept.

On the technical side, when I'm ready to produce, I will first record myself using my laptop web camera in a program like QuickTime where I can capture myself speaking through the whole video. I usually will include some footage of myself speaking, but even if I don't intersperse footage of myself, then having my audio recorded first usually helps me orient what visuals I should produce after that.

After I have recorded myself, I take that file and upload it to a movie-making program, like iMovie. In iMovie, it's very easy to upload a video file and then add your visual assets afterward. I typically use my scripting work to guide how I search for images to upload and pull into the video timeline. Sometimes, I'll create my visual in a slideware program and then take a screenshot of the slide to turn the slide into an image file (like a JPEG) that I can easily upload and place into the timeline of my iMovie video. The process of making the visuals typically takes me the longest because sometimes, once I see the video file in the video editing software, I have an idea to incorporate more visuals than I had initially planned. I find I really do have to see myself on video and listen to myself speak before I know where the best place is to create visual markers throughout.

When I'm feeling like my video production is complete in iMovie, I export the video file in a generic video format (like an MP4 file) and then upload that video into a video storage and distribution platform, like YouTube. Platforms like YouTube include good accessibility, captioning, and transcription tools that I lean heavily on in order to ensure that the video I am creating will be accessible to all learners.

Michael's Process

The centerpiece of my process is Keynote, to create slides, and Camtasia, to record and edit videos. I start with pencil and paper. Just a simple list of the main ideas I want to present in the video. Next, I create a set of slides in Keynote, just text to start with, one slide for each idea. Then I start to think about visuals: What is the best way to visualize each idea? I find photos or create simple shapes or graphics for each idea. At this point, I have a working set of slides that captures the main ideas for the video. I click through the slides a couple times, adding and adjusting slides as needed to flesh out the story I am presenting in the video. For a 5-minute video, I may create 10 or 12 slides.

The slides form the backbone of the video and now I can draft a script of what I plan to say in the audio voice-over. I read through the script a couple times to work out the timing. Usually, the script needs to be edited to make it fit in the allotted time.

With the slides and script complete, I am ready to record. I'll usually do a dry run first and record it, to listen to how the pacing and timing work, and adjust as needed. Then I record the video and audio at the same time. If I misspoke at some point, I could just continue and edit out the mistakes later. Then I save and export the final file and post it to YouTube (usually). I edit the captions and post a transcript (usually as a PDF). One more test run to make sure the final file, captions, and transcripts work for everyone, and then the video is ready to share with the learners!

Putting It Together

You will notice several key differences in our personal processes. Jenae starts with the words, drafting a script first and then a rough storyboard. Michael usually starts with an outline and then creates a

---

WHICH SOFTWARE SHOULD I USE?

The choice of video editing software can lead you down a rabbit-hole. There are many options, and designers can have strong opinions about them. There is no one ideal product to use for producing videos. We have a few recommendations for tools based on examples that are currently in use as of 2023.

- **iMovie:** This is a free, easy-to-use video editing and creation tool that's available to Mac users. Most Mac laptops already have iMovie built in. The interface is basically "drag-and-drop" and allows users to import lots of video elements, such as additional sounds, music, and images, into a video timeline.

- **Camtasia:** A relatively inexpensive piece of instructional video software developed by TechSmith, Camtasia is a good choice if you would like to do more sophisticated video editing than iMovie and if you plan to incorporate a lot of screenshots into your video. Camtasia is a tool designed specifically for educational contexts, as well, so their website has lots of resources designed for people who are creating instructional videos.

- **Iorad:** With a monthly payment fee, Iorad is also built for designers making tutorial videos. That means step-by-step instructions are auto-generated and automated voice-overs are available. (Yes, you can have a voice-over without using your own voice!) This tool's features are largely intended to be used in specific technical tutorial contexts, so if that's

slide deck to use like a storyboard. Whether you start with words or visuals, at the end of the process, you will need a script, the visuals you want to include on-screen, and the software you will use to record and edit the final video product.

Both processes illustrate a few key principles: that producing a video doesn't have to be incredibly technical and time-consuming, but that it should be done systematically. Knowing which pieces you need to create, and in which order you need to create them, can and should make a tremendous difference in organizing and feeling less stressed about the creation of your final product.

There are options beyond what the two of us have done, however. As technologies change and access to multimedia production becomes increasingly accessible, more options may continue to open up, and it's worth being aware what some of those options are so that you can make a more intentional choice aligned with your own skills, experiences, and preferences.

largely what you're designing for your course, this more specialized tool may reduce some of the time and labor in the video production process.

- **Descript:** It's a "freemium" tool (i.e., a tool where some features are free and some require subscription), Descript automatically generates transcripts that can be useful for creating screencast scripts. While the automated transcripts are not 100% accurate, they can make it much easier to edit transcripts later and more quickly generate the content and scripts needed for screencast videos.

- **Adobe Premiere:** This is an industry-leading solution for creating video, and it should really be considered if you'd like to develop a deeper career in video production and editing. Adobe Premiere is the expert's solution, which means you will have more detailed, technical features for making videos than any of the other tools we've mentioned so far. But with more features come more of a learning curve.

- **Mobile Options:** You could easily create a video on your iPhone or Android phone. Both devices include applications by default that allow for high-fidelity recording. However, editing options on mobile devices lack sophistication. Social media apps like TikTok and Snapchat have video editors that allow for some fairly elaborate effects, but using apps like these may make your video look less professional and more informal.

Think Through Your Final Product

As you start to pull together your script, visuals, and other content for your video, imagine how you want the final product to look. As you think through the video, begin to imagine a rhythm and flow for the video. Vary the images on-screen and use different types of visuals to create breaks between sections or main ideas (see Figures 7.1 and 7.2).

FIGURE 7.1
Jenae includes not only an image of herself speaking, but also an icon to illustrate a concept she's speaking about in the video.

FIGURE 7.2
Michael uses a book as a prop to illustrate and gesture toward a key reference used in his class.

"Talking head" segments work well at the beginning of a video, to establish presence and connect learners to the person behind the learning content. But keep these segments short: learners tire quickly of watching you talk! Save the talking heads for the beginning and end of the video. Title slides or subtitle pages work well to create visual breaks between segments of a video (see Figures 7.3 and 7.4). Learners can scrub through the video to find sections quickly. Title slides can be used as a type of visual punctuation between main ideas and help to create a sense of visual timing and rhythm.

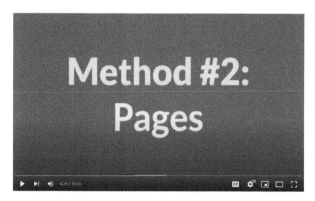

FIGURE 7.3
This instructional video from Jenae shows how she uses a bold and simple transition to move from describing one workflow to another.

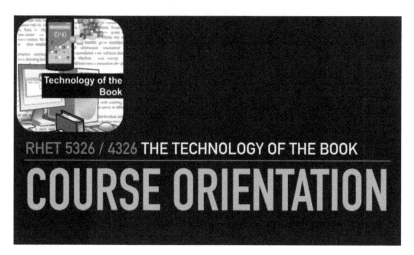

FIGURE 7.4
Michael's instructional video uses bright colors and clear color contrast to create an introductory graphic that opens up his course video. He consistently uses this graphic throughout his courses to create clear branding and orientation to his class.

"Visual tours" or walk-through segments can be used to demonstrate how to navigate or access content on an instructional website (see Figure 7.5). Many video editors include visual callouts or highlights like the yellow circle in Figure 7.6. When you are creating a walk-through or demo, be sure to move the cursor slowly and describe verbally what you are doing on-screen.

NOTE DON'T WIGGLE THE CURSOR!

Some learning designers will use rapid cursor movements to highlight things on-screen. Avoid doing this! Rapid cursor movements are highly distracting and often irritating. Use verbal descriptions to indicate where you want learners' attention to go. Don't say "As you can see here," but rather use explicit words ("in the upper-left corner"). Verbal descriptions are much more accessible for learners with visual disabilities.

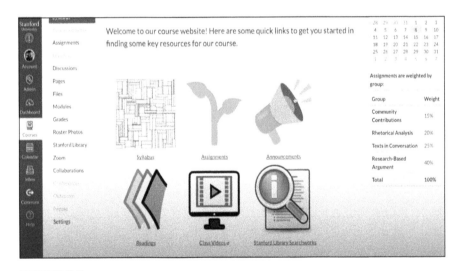

FIGURE 7.5
Jenae's video shows how the different buttons on the home page work, and it orients users to what can be found in the left-hand menu for the course.

FIGURE 7.6

Michael's video shows one of the content pages of the course website he designed, highlighting what students can find when they click different menu items.

Three Pathways to Produce Videos

There are three options for video production that learning designers should consider, particularly if they are producing a video without the support of a professional video producer; however, these tips and this process can be approached with greater technical precision and complexity when you're in consultation with a designated video producer or graphic designer. Choosing which of these pathways to select may also depend on how frequently you need to redo or rethink the content in your videos. Some videos, by nature of their content, may have a longer "shelf life" than others and, as such, may benefit from more intensive video production workflows to produce higher quality content. But these three pathways will give you some ideas about how to create an effective instructional video without requiring a specialist's knowledge in video production.

Option 1: Make Your Video Entirely in a Slideware Tool

The easiest option to create a video is by using the same kind of slideware tools, like Microsoft PowerPoint, Google Slides, or Keynote, that you might use for a live presentation. Everything from your storyboard to your visuals and even your script can be produced all within the space of a slideware tool. Many slideware tools now even include screen-recording options built in, and the final output of the video file can often be saved within the same slideware option.

If your slideware tool of choice does not include a screen-recording option, you can find a screen-recording tool either built into your machine (for example, QuickTime on a Mac or Microsoft Stream on Windows), or you can download one online (see Loom, OBS, and Screencast-O-Matic). To capture effects like music or your voice-over, you could play any audio clips directly from your computer speakers and capture the audio from your speakers. The audio quality may not sound quite as strong with this approach, but in a pinch, and if you're trying to take the easiest production option possible, it will work.

Option 2: Make Your Video in a Drag-and-Drop Tool

If you want to be able to edit your video more easily than with a simple screen-recording tool in your slideware program, you might consider using a drag-and-drop tool to create your video. Drag-and-drop interfaces enable users to easily add the components of a video (i.e., images, music, and voice-over narration) to a timeline to generate a video. There are a lot of variations of drag-and-drop video editing tools out there, all of which aim to simplify the video editing process from the highly technical and elaborate tools that professional video editors may use.

For example, if you are using designated eLearning software, such as Articulate 360 or Adobe Captivate, you should be able to create some video content directly within the platform. Both Articulate 360 and Adobe Captivate enable users to create simple "slide-style" videos where they can drag-and-drop photos and illustrations into a timeline and add music to the background.

If you are not using a designated eLearning software suite to create your eLearning content, you might turn to browser-based, drag-and-drop video creation tools, such as Adobe Express and Canva, both of which are considered "freemium" tools. For example, you might only be able to create a video that's less than three minutes long or the video may include a watermark or branding from the tool. So, bear in mind that if you have not already invested in using proprietary eLearning software, you may still need to invest a bit into video production software to be free of some constraining conditions for making your videos.

All these tools will require some learning. Designated eLearning platforms, especially like Articulate and Captivate, tend to include extensive technical documentation on how and when to use the features they make available. However, the more functionality within the tool that's available, the more sophisticated and varied your end product will be. Consider what the vision for your video is and whether the features available within some drag-and-drop tools will align with your video's needs.

Option 3: Make Your Video in a Designated Consumer Video Editing Tool

If you really want to have a lot of control over your final video product and you're willing to learn how to use a video editor with full functionality, consider making your video with a downloadable designated consumer video editing tool, such as Camtasia, Shotcut, or if you truly want to learn a professional-quality video editing tool, Adobe Premiere. These tools are built to have stand-alone functionality, and they will rarely include templates or full drag-and-drop interfaces. However, most consumer video editing tools include extensive documentation and how-to guides to help get you up to speed, even though you will have to learn some new ways of making and doing things.

Professional video editing tools will give you a lot more control over your end product. Some learning designers may find that they are willing to give up some control to save time. But other learning designers may want full control over the end product and will want to make more precise revisions without working within a premade template or being limited to using premade assets, such as royalty-free music or images included within a drag-and-drop interface. Basically, the more choices you have in your video creation process, the more work it will be for you to produce the video.

A skill you will need to develop if you are using a professional video editing tool is the ability to organize and import all of your assets for your video in advance. That means that all images, music, or audio tracks will need to be produced separately before getting combined and imported into the video editing tool of your choice. This might be exactly what you want to do, especially if in the planning process, you built out your assets already or had visions of creating assets that were highly specific or customized to your course. However, if you are envisioning a video that would primarily be made up of stock images or generic photos, then the drag-and-drop option may provide you with enough functionality.

A benefit to using a professional video editing tool is that you have more options for the file form in exporting your video content as well. Most professional video editing tools will allow you to export your videos in multiple file formats, which would give you options for how and where your final video product will be shared. Sometimes, the drag-and-drop video editing tools have fewer choices for the output or file format for your final product, which could limit how and where the video you've produced can be used. In particular, if you're building a video within a particular eLearning platform, it's unlikely that you'll have many options for exporting or sharing your video outside of the platform.

Learning some basic video editing skills and working through the learning curve will be worth it in the long run if you anticipate that making videos will be a regular part of how you create content for online learning experiences in the future. As with everything else, the more practice you get in using a new tool, the more adept you'll become.

Recording Audio Voice-Over

One of the most underrated components of video production is taking the time to record high-quality audio for the video. It's easy to get so focused on the visuals that you lose sight of the audio. However, the vast majority of instructional videos produced will have spoken audio content. After you've decided on your tools and workflow for producing your full video, consider a few principles that will help you create higher quality voice-over or narration audio.

- **Use a good microphone.** Bad audio is hard on listeners. Background noise and tinny-sounding voices can ruin a good presentation. You don't want audio that sounds like it was recorded in a submarine. Do a test for echoes or feedback. A good microphone in a quiet room is necessary to achieve good results for your listeners.

- **Smile as you speak (yes, really!).** If you are recording audio where you want to sound upbeat, try smiling as you talk. You can hear the difference when someone is speaking with or without a smile. There is a strong connection between your body and your brain, so the more that you can cue your body to sound "happy," the happier you will sound.

- **Practice.** With practice, you can almost memorize a short script and make it sound smoother and more natural. Record yourself doing your practice runs so that you can listen to your practice takes and note where you might want to speed up, slow down, enunciate more clearly, or sound more (or less!) energetic.

- **Edit your final audio.** It's usually easier and faster to edit out slips or misspoken words than to re-record the whole script. Software like Adobe Audition or Audacity can allow you to splice in short pieces and improve the audio quality by masking background noise.

- **Include transcripts.** Always include and link to a transcript. This should be easy to do if you've scripted out your audio anyway.

You don't have to sound like an audiobook narrator or a podcast host to record effective audio. Aim for making yourself sound like an approachable human being more than anything else! Enthusiasm and energy in your voice can make up for any lack of "voice actor" polish.

Selecting and Identifying Music

If you've ever walked into a store without music playing, you might notice how strange it feels to be inside the store. The same thing goes for any kind of video content: having a video with nothing to listen to right away can make watching that video feel alienating and empty. At a minimum, if you include some intro and outro music to your video, it will help set the tone and create auditory interest in the video.

Tone and Feeling

At this point in your process, you should have a clear sense of the purpose of your video. Many instructional videos include music that is upbeat and uplifting, but not exactly a full-on funky party, to encourage engagement and to energize their viewers. But there may be moments when something more contemplative or calming is more appropriate. As long as you approach your musical selection by first imagining what you want to evoke in your viewer, it will be easier to narrow down the extensive field of musical options.

You might try playing the audio you're considering for a friend or family member. Pick a few people to play your music for, in fact, and ask them what it makes them think of or what it evokes for them. The information you get from others should help corroborate how you're experiencing the impact of the video.

Understanding Legal Music Choices

Before you get your heart set on using a particular song for your video, make absolutely certain that you're searching for music within designated stock audio libraries. Just as you have to assume that any image you find online is copyrighted, the music you select should be considered copyrighted as well, unless it includes a special, designated license, like a Creative Commons license, to indicate otherwise.

Popular music is copyrighted, and if you include the full length of a popular song—or any song that has been produced within the last 75 years—you must pay royalties to the artist. It is generally a safer bet from a legal perspective to select music that has been explicitly composed either for free and reusable purposes or that is being sold specifically for instructional or commercial contexts. It is a general courtesy to credit any music that you use in a video somewhere, even if the song has been designated by the artist as freely usable, reusable, and remixable in a variety of contexts.

The fair use clause in American copyright law indicates that a short snippet of a popular song can be used in a video for free. A "short" snippet is typically defined as including 30 seconds or less of a popular song. Using a snippet of that length will likely not be very worthwhile in the context of an instructional video unless you're making a very specific reference to a highly recognizable song. Even then, think carefully about how important it is to use a highly recognizable or popular song.

Think of music largely as "mood-setting." Fortunately, there are a lot of royalty-free music options out there that can explicitly help set a mood.

Sound Effects

Other sound effects beyond music, such as transition sounds between key visuals or a noise like a cymbal crash for emphasis, can have a powerful impact for helping viewers distinguish between different pieces of content. You can often find audio clips for sound effects in royalty-free music libraries alongside fuller pieces of music. If you are producing your video in a slideware tool, some slideware tools include the option to trigger audio effects on a keyboard command or along with a visual animation. These might all be options to consider in some very specific instructional circumstances.

Sound effects should be used sparingly, however. Sound effects that go beyond music or your voice can sound cartoonish or disorienting for the viewer. Some sound effects, such as a horn or a siren, have certain cultural connotations that may have very different meanings for different viewers. For example, a siren for an American viewer may connote the feeling of looking for an ambulance; however, an ambulance sound in other countries is often a bit different. Regardless, you do not want cultural connotation for particular noises or sounds to be a distraction from your content and goals.

It can be helpful to mix up what your viewer is hearing and add in some sound effects for emphasis. But still, be cautious: sound effects should really only be used at moments when you think that music or your voice alone will not have the impact needed.

Make Your Video Accessible

As you produce your video, think about ways to make the video accessible: writing your script, for example, will help you generate a transcript and captions for your video as you go. However, the narration for the video is not the only opportunity to make the content accessible. As you engage in your final video production, you'll want to think about the full range of ways to make the multimedia experience accessible for everyone.

Writing Audio and Image Descriptions for the Transcript

Include image and audio descriptions in the body of the transcript file. For example, if your video begins with introductory music, write an audio description at the start of your transcript that describes the sound and feeling of the music that is being played. You might derive some inspiration for how to describe music by watching a movie with the closed captions turned on. You'll see that closed captions typically include descriptions of music like, "Peppy, upbeat music," which will indicate to deaf or hard-of-hearing listeners that there is a certain tone or mood being captured before the video even begins.

Similarly, as images appear on-screen, be sure that the transcript includes what the viewer is looking at as they're watching. That way, if a viewer is only looking at the transcript, and not watching the video itself, they can know what they are supposed to be seeing. The transcript becomes a useful and essential tool not only for disabled viewers, but also for viewers who may struggle with low quality or inconsistent Wi-Fi bandwidth that could make accessing video unstable.

Designing Captions

If you are uploading a video to a major video streaming service, such as YouTube or Vimeo, you will likely not have control over the appearance of your captions. However, if you are using a video distribution tool that does not include a closed captioning interface for displaying the captions, you may be asked to manually modify or add the captions yourself. Be mindful of the color and appearance of the captions; some captions can be impossible to read, for example, if the captions are in white text and are appearing on a white background. Whenever possible, attempt to align the background colors or images with the color or appearance of the text in the captions you're producing.

Make Each Video Count

Videos are a powerful, engaging, and immersive media choice for learners to engage with content throughout your course. It will be tempting to go overboard and rely on videos for everything. Instead, think carefully about the roles that different kinds of video will play in your course. The types of videos we've described here in this chapter (and Chapter 6, "Planning Videos") require a lot of time, attention, and focus to produce effectively. You may find it valuable to occasionally create one-off or informal videos to communicate a key message or build community (see Chapter 9, "Building Connections Among Learners," for more information). But on the whole, as you approach your entire video planning and production strategy, be intentional about where your final produced videos wind up in the course. There is such a thing as too much video. Your videos will have more power and impact if you vary them alongside text, images, and other interactions in your course that are well-aligned with the balance of interactions that your learners will have.

Takeaways

- **Define your production process.** This process should be simple and repeatable. Having a repeatable workflow process will let you focus on the content of the video rather than the technical details of the software.

- **Show yourself on-screen, but only for short segments.** Limit your screen time to the beginning and end of a video.

- **Create title slides to break up segments.** Titles and subtitle slides help learners find information and navigate through your video.

- **Make your video accessible.** Create a transcript with audio and image descriptions and make sure that your captions are clear and readable.

CHAPTER 8

Facilitating Live Webinar Presentations

Requesting and receiving someone's undivided attention in real time is asking for a lot; however, undivided attention is what most live webinar events, or live meetings over Zoom, Google Meet, or other video conferencing platforms, actually demand. It might not sound like such a big deal given how ubiquitous and popular webinars have become in today's educational and training landscape. But offering a webinar is not nearly as easy as opening a meeting room and talking into a camera, at least if you're going to lead a webinar that really takes full advantage of the tremendous "ask" you've made on someone else's time.

Maybe you've experienced "Zoom fatigue" after attending a live webinar event or course. This experience usually refers to a kind of achy, hazy feeling that people get when they've been staring at a screen (and their own faces) for hours without engaging very much. That's usually the consequence of a poorly designed webinar where people's time and energy aren't as respected as they could be. In a bad webinar, a facilitator simply drones on about a topic, trying to cram as much content as they can deliver into a short period of time.

If a bad webinar is led by a talking head who keeps you captive and bored, then a good webinar is led by a facilitator who is organizing a lively conversation. The primary benefit of delivering content *live* is that people can engage with other people in real time. Part of showing the kind of respect that transforms a webinar from "blah" to "great" is welcoming the real, live people's real, live questions, ideas, and comments.

Just as the whole learning experience you're designing needs to have clear outcomes and objectives—things that your learners will *do* with the information—so too must any single webinar or live presentation.

A WEBINAR THAT WORKED

Take a live presentation that Jenae attended as an example: The presenter's goal was to help the audience understand the best ways to work with neurodiverse learners when designing a workshop or a course. In order to do that, the presenter gave three clear outcomes for the live presentation:

- Design activities and assignments that are inclusive of neurodiverse learner needs.
- Understand the spectrum of neurodiverse approaches to learning.
- Adopt language for course materials that demonstrates inclusion of and toward neurodiverse learner needs.

In order to achieve these outcomes, the presenter asked the live audience to engage in several activities throughout the webinar. To begin, she asked audience members to respond to prompts and questions in a live chat space to assess audience understanding of various neurodiverse conditions. Then, at the midpoint of the presentation, she gave a writing prompt to the audience members to help them craft a statement for their course about including neurodiverse learners. And by the end of the presentation, she asked the participants to contribute to a shared spreadsheet where participants could enter their class activity ideas and assignments into different fields to create a crowd-sourced list of inclusive activity and assignment ideas.

In this case, the presenter was intentional about what made a live presentation special: the ability to engage with individuals in real time and offer them guidance, support, and coaching through the process of learning new information. And while the presenter also did some lecturing and content sharing, she also effectively helped learners do something with the information she shared with deliberate activity breaks and engagements throughout.

What Makes a Webinar Unique

In order to identify what might make a live presentation more worthwhile for your learners than a prerecorded video, it's important to think first about the unique qualities of a live webinar presentation experience.

In a webinar, participants have agency about how and where they engage. Unlike a live, on-site presentation, where participants would likely have the social expectation that they would remain seated and in one place for a set period of time, webinar participants can tune in while on a walk, driving a car, or folding laundry in their living room. If you try to control the movements and engagements of a webinar participant, it's, at best, a losing proposition and, at worst, a great way to alienate people.

Take the case of Jenae's mother, who felt incredibly frustrated by the restrictive rules in a professional development webinar she attended for her work as a therapist. While attending the webinar, she had her camera off, and the facilitator sent her a private message to turn her camera on. She immediately felt embarrassed because she had just finished exercising, was sweaty, and was listening to the webinar while cleaning her floors. She turned the camera on, but felt self-conscious the entire time. She decided to leave early and not return to the webinar again. Even though she was still interested in the material, the experience made her uncomfortable enough not to bother returning for the next session. Don't make participants feel resentful or uncomfortable like this. Instead, be flexible about how the participants choose to engage. It's their learning experience after all.

In a webinar, participants also have multiple means of "speaking up." When you are gathering in an on-site environment, most participants will demonstrate engagement by speaking. However, in a webinar, participants can turn on their microphones and speak in a live context, or they can just as easily type their comments in a live chat space. Some webinar facilitators may want to control the channels for participant engagement. However, trying to "lock down" what participants can and can't use may make people feel overly controlled and without options, especially if they're joining in from a slower internet connection, are not in a quiet space, or simply don't have a quality microphone to use. As a facilitator, you should orient users to all of the available options for engaging and help participants understand what those options mean rather than limiting or eliminating particular channels for communication.

As you're designing your webinar materials, bear in mind that participants can save information from the webinar easily with screenshots and recordings. In an on-site learning context, participants may take photos of the presentation or use a device to record, but capturing components of the presentation is even easier to do online with a screenshot and the capacity to record often embedded within the webinar application itself. While some webinar platforms may give facilitators the option to restrict recording, it is almost impossible to shut down the ability to capture parts of a screen without using incredibly invasive (and, frankly, unethical) surveillance technology. Be judicious about what you share in a webinar. If there's something you really don't want webinar participants to screenshot, save, or share, you should request that participants sign a waiver or other documentation prior to attending the webinar. The choices available and the options created can make webinars a much more inviting and inclusive way for all people to get access to information wherever they are so long as you embrace the options and plan ahead.

Organizing Webinar Materials

The key to any good live event is preparation. The more that you organize the flow of your live webinar event up front, the more confident you will feel and the more prepared you will be to respond to live engagements from the audience. It's especially helpful if you're feeling nervous about technical troubles that might throw off your entire experience. While you can assume your audience will give you the benefit of the doubt, even if you can't share your screen immediately or your internet connection glitches for a moment, it will feel better to work through those challenging moments if you have a clear plan in mind. You'll feel a lot more present with the webinar participants when you're feeling like you have a good handle on what you want to share and why.

You can prioritize what to say or do during a live presentation if you can come up with three things you want your participants to remember by the time the webinar is over. Think about how you'll advance those key three ideas throughout the webinar. Perhaps you can divide your webinar into three parts, one for each idea. You could also consider how the three ideas get interwoven throughout your webinar at repeated points.

Then imagine your presentation like a story arc (see Figure 8.1). One clear structure for the webinar that participants will recognize is a classic story arc: start with an introduction, create some rising action, and then at the halfway point, have a clear "climax" or high point of the workshop. End the presentation by winding down with some concluding points and takeaways. You can even be very explicit with your participants that you're taking this approach. Storytelling is compelling, and the more you can draw upon patterns that participants will recognize, like a classic story arc, the more they'll be able to focus on the content itself.

FIGURE 8.1

Understanding the typical arc for a story can help learning designers create a compelling webinar experience that engages participants.

After you've settled on your areas of focus and the general flow of your ideas, create a "run-of-show" document to help you keep track of how long certain components of your presentation will take. That way, you can estimate roughly how long each component of your webinar will be so that you don't over (or under) prepare the activities and the content. We encourage chunking your webinar content up into short bursts of time; think of your webinar in terms of 5–10-minute segments, if possible. Bear in mind that when a participant is online, their focus will probably drift easily to other applications or contexts. Dividing up your webinar into short time segments will ensure that no one activity or listening session in your webinar takes too long and that you are creating ample opportunities for participants to pause, ask questions, and engage with each other throughout the shared time they have.

We've imagined an example webinar run-of-show for an hour-long webinar (see Table 8.1). In our example, we've focused on four types of engagements we want participants to alternate between: facilitator-to-participant social engagement (indicated in yellow), facilitator-to-participant content delivery (indicated in blue), participant-to-participant engagement (indicated in green), and full group breaks (indicated in red). In webinars we facilitate, we really like to be intentional about the audience's role and take advantage of multiple ways to bring out their real-time engagement.

We find it useful to have links or resources prepared up front, especially if we're asking participants to navigate to resources outside of the webinar screen or window itself. For example, if we want to give participants access to the slides that we're sharing in the webinar tool, we make sure that the slides themselves are online in a document-sharing or distribution tool, like Google Slides, Canva, or Microsoft PowerPoint online. We may also facilitate activities where participants take polls or write in a shared Google document or live Microsoft Word document. Those activities require that participants temporarily leave the webinar window to access those documents and be able to work and scroll between them during the webinar time itself (kind of like using handouts during a live, on-site session).

In some instances, there are multiple facilitators in a webinar who may be able to play different roles. For example, one person might be the "emcee" who speaks during the session and manages the overall time. Another person might be the "chat monitor," who makes sure that all of the information shared verbally is also shared by text in the chatbox space. If this is the case, the run-of-show can also be a good space to delegate who will be doing which tasks during the webinar. That said, it is doable to have one person take on these multiple roles, but the more roles that one person is required to do, the more detailed and organized the run-of-show should be to ensure that materials are prepared in an easily accessible and orderly way.

TABLE 8.1   EXAMPLE WEBINAR RUN-OF-SHOW

Time	Activity	Notes	Links/Resources
9:00–9:05 A.M.	Welcome. Orientation to the agenda. Chat introduction with participants.	Orient participants to the tools for engagement during the webinar with options for engagement.	Link to slide deck.
9:05–9:10 A.M.	Review webinar objectives and outcomes. Introduce small group activity to review and discuss case studies.	Remind participants that they can access the slide deck to read the small group activity instructions, but you are taking this time to review the instructions in advance.	Link to Google Docs for small group activity engagement.
9:10–9:25 A.M.	Participants are in small breakout groups to discuss case studies.	Ask the person whose birthday is coming up the soonest to be responsible for taking notes in their small group (even though every participant has a link to contribute).	
9:25–9:30 A.M.	Review findings from breakout groups. Discuss overall patterns and trends from the Google Docs notes document.	Give options for how participants can share group findings (for example, can raise a hand to speak on the mic or contribute in the chat).	Link to Google Docs again in case anyone missed it.
9:30–9:35 A.M.	5-minute break	Put up a countdown timer on slides.	
9:35–9:50 A.M.	Introduce research to back up findings from case studies.		Link to any studies/resources cited.
9:50–9:55 A.M.	5-minute individual reflection. Ask participants what they gained from exploring the case studies and how they'll apply findings from the case studies to their work.		Link to online pinboard where participants can post their reflections if they'd like to share anonymously.
9:55–10:00 A.M.	Closing remarks. Point to further resources if participants would like to learn more.		Link to websites with more resources and send link to slide deck again.

Creating an Engaging Webinar

As the example run-of-show suggests, keeping the activities varied and lively is critical to creating a high-quality webinar. While you don't want to overwhelm your participants with a huge array of options, you also don't want them to get bored.

The sweet spot, really, is engaging with participants in at least two different ways. Perhaps you can invite them to respond to a prompt in the chat and ask them to add a sticky-note to a digital pinboard, like Google Jamboard. Maybe you can ask them to type content into a row in a shared collaborative spreadsheet, like Google Sheets, and respond to an anonymous poll, such as the polling feature built into Zoom. There are a lot of choices here, but think about which choices best match the ways that you'd like participants to demonstrate their knowledge, ask questions, or be in conversation with each other. We've organized a few different options to help you align possible webinar engagement strategies with situations where it might be best to deploy this strategy, and then we've listed current tools that may make this strategy work (see Table 8.2).

TABLE 8.2 WEBINAR ENGAGEMENT STRATEGIES

Webinar Engagement Strategy	When to Use This Strategy	Tools to Support This Strategy (Current as of 2022)
Participants respond to a question or a prompt in a live chatbox space.	When you want to see a variety of opinions on a topic, gauge understanding of a topic, or learn about the backgrounds and experiences of people in the webinar.	Most webinar tools (for example, Zoom, Cisco Webex, Google Meet, Microsoft Teams) have a chat feature built in that can be used for this strategy.
Participants complete a poll.	When you want to "take the temperature" and get a sense about aggregated responses to a particular set of questions. When you want to get a feel for how much shared knowledge the group has on a particular topic.	Google Forms Microsoft Forms Poll Everywhere Mentimeter

continued

TABLE 8.2 CONTINUED

Webinar Engagement Strategy	When to Use This Strategy	Tools to Support This Strategy (Current as of 2022)
Participants create a digital "pinboard" or "whiteboard" where they can add a short note, idea, or link to a resource.	When you want your participants to aggregate multiple, distinct resources into one place. When you want to brainstorm ideas as a group or engage in a design thinking exercise.	Google Jamboard Microsoft Whiteboard Padlet
Participants contribute to a shared document or spreadsheet.	When you want your participants to create a collective resource where ideas might be shared or overlapping. When you want your participants to cocreate a document or a resource.	Google Docs Google Sheets Microsoft Word or Excel Online
Participants annotate a PDF or a website together in real time.	When you want your participants to read something together and leave notes that they can see directly on the text or website that you'd like for them to explore.	Hypothes.is Scrible
Participants talk in small groups and work together.	When you want your participants to have a conversation about a particular topic or to problem solve and brainstorm together.	Zoom Breakout Rooms Engageli Breakout Tables
Participants leave questions in a question bank throughout the webinar.	When you want your participants to ask open-ended questions throughout the webinar both for "Q&A" time at the end and to respond to questions throughout the webinar time.	Most webinar tools (for example, Zoom, Cisco Webex, Google Meet, Microsoft Teams) have a "Q&A" feature built in for this strategy. However, some polling tools also have Q&A features, including: Poll Everywhere Mentimeter

Beyond creating engaging activities during the webinar, you'll also want to think through a pacing for your webinar that gives participants plenty of room to get up from their seats, stretch, take a break, or simply look away from their screens for a moment. Variety doesn't just mean doing a bunch of different things. Recognize the demand this event requires for participants and give them the space to breathe accordingly. Everyone will appreciate it.

Creating Webinar Materials

Most webinar facilitators will create a slide deck to provide visuals during the live event. These visuals can help reinforce the organizational structure of the presentation while also providing images, diagrams, and graphs that highlight key points and messages in your content. Many of the tips for creating visuals for videos apply to presentations as well, with perhaps a few key differences.

For a webinar, you'll want to use the slides to provide instruction/direction for any activities (see Figure 8.2). That might mean creating slides throughout your webinar that have timers embedded to show how much time is left for a given activity or that simply include an amount of time that participants can expect to spend thinking about or doing something.

FIGURE 8.2

Some examples that include activity instructions in the slides themselves; the screenshots directly embedded in the slides illustrate where participants can find the information they need to engage with the activity.

It might also mean having one slide include a larger block of text that explains what they should be doing with the time at that moment (see Figure 8.3). That way, participants don't need to rely simply upon listening for any instructions; the slides can reinforce what they should be doing or paying attention to at any given moment.

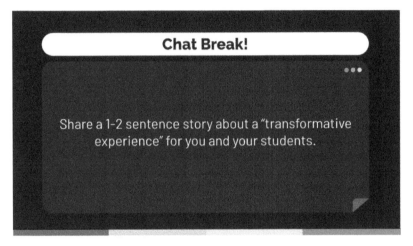

FIGURE 8.3
You can display instructions on a slide very simply. The words "Chat Break" at the top of the slide indicate that participants will use the chat to respond to the prompt in the center of the slide.

That said, keep text to a minimum for anything that's not an instruction or direction. When you are delivering content during your webinar, it's important to follow the same principles of visual design that you would use when producing prerecorded videos (see Figure 8.3). Rely upon images, diagrams, and graphics rather than writing long essays or full sentences on your slides so that participants don't have to read and listen at the same time (see Figure 8.4).

FIGURE 8.4

A collage of simple images shows illustrations of what different methods of reading can look like, designed for a webinar presentation on how to teach approaches to reading.

Since the slide deck is such an important organizational and visual tool for your webinar, you'll want to be sure that you're making your visuals as easy to read and access for your audience as possible. Some visual designers argue that using a dark background for your slides with a lighter font (for example, a black background with white font) is easier to read for a longer period of time on a screen than a lighter background with a darker font (a white background with a black font). While you are not limited to using black and white as your color scheme, think about how you can pair dark backgrounds with lighter text or font colors throughout so that you are not straining your participants' eyes and, more importantly, you're not creating content that is inaccessible entirely to an audience member who may have partial or full color blindness.

You might also think of the slide deck itself as a valuable parting resource for participants to use or engage with after the webinar is over. There's a lot to take in during a live webinar presentation and, chances are, your participants aren't going to catch everything they might want to learn about in real time. Consider creating an online folder (perhaps stored in a cloud storage program like Google Drive or Dropbox) with materials you'd like for participants to access after the webinar. If you are concerned about the sharing or circulation of your own intellectual property, you can make the materials password protected and prevent users from downloading or exporting the content from the folder.

Preparing for Your Webinar

You've got your materials completed and your webinar is planned. It's time to prepare just a little bit more and get comfortable with some of the tools and techniques that you'll use as you speak to participants live.

Start by learning which unique tools may be available within the webinar platform you're using. Most webinar platforms have a few special features that can enhance interactions, such as participant "reactions" (where participants give "thumbs ups" or display other emojis on-screen when they so choose) or participant "breakout rooms" where participants can be put into smaller groups. These aren't ubiquitous across all platforms, however, so learn what's at your disposal, both so you can be aware of how you might structure interactions, but also so that you know what particular features are called (and what they do) to help participants with some technical troubleshooting.

After you're familiar with all of the tools and features, then give all of the technical details a test run. Just as you might do a "mic check" if you were to speak in an auditorium, make sure that you know exactly where the audio and video for your webinar is sourcing from. For example, if you are using an external microphone or web camera to improve the audio and visual quality of your webinar, make sure that your webinar platform is using your microphone and your web camera as the source for your audio and video output.

Part of your "mic check" should also include a "desktop" check, especially if you are going to be sharing your screen during your webinar. If you have any digital handouts or resources you're going to share, get them queued up (you should have them listed in your "run-of-show" document anyway). Plus, you don't want to be caught unaware with something distracting on your desktop when it comes time to share your screen. Close all of your extra tabs, folders, or documents that may be irrelevant to your webinar.

These steps should ultimately not be very time-consuming. You might even turn these steps into a short checklist to consult prior to your webinar so that you don't forget some of the small details and pieces that can make your webinar experience run smoothly.

Rehearsing Your Webinar

Just as you'd record and practice how you'd like to speak for a prerecorded video, you'll want to do the same kind of practice run and rehearsal for a live event. Unlike a prerecorded video, you won't be able to replicate the entire webinar experience in advance, since (hopefully!) you're preparing materials that are responsive to a live audience. However, referring to your "run-of-show" document, where you've created a map of how long you roughly want to spend in each part of your webinar can still be helpful to practice.

You might practice the chunks of your webinar where you are speaking without engaging and give yourself some time to practice moving between different applications on your computer if you will be moving between the webinar program and other documents or applications. Basically, the more moving parts you've built into your run-of-show, the more that you'll want to give yourself the opportunity to practice.

For example, Michael once gave a live webinar presentation on how to use a tool called Camtasia to edit video. To prepare for this webinar, he hopped onto the webinar platform and loaded up his version of Camtasia and practiced editing a video clip on Camtasia in real time. Before his webinar, he already had a practice video edited, and he knew how to move nimbly between the webinar platform and Camtasia. If you're going to be engaging in a similar kind of demonstration of an additional tool, you may feel more at ease for the live webinar if you similarly prepare your usage of external tools in advance.

If you've got a little extra time, ask a friend to join your webinar platform. It can be helpful to see, even if just for a few minutes, what it looks like to have another participant join in on the webinar with you. Ask them to use some of the features you're asking the webinar participants to use so that you get a feel for what it looks like.

Bear in mind that any "rehearsal" of your webinar is not going to be reflective of the live experience. Inherently, live experiences will include some twists, turns, and unexpected occurrences. But most facilitators feel like they can be more present and engaged with their audience if they're not stumbling over their own materials or forgetting what they want to say. And that's the primary purpose of rehearsal: to make you as comfortable as you can be with the content you need to deliver so that you can really be present and enjoy yourself for the live experience.

Delivering Webinar Materials

With all of your preparation and practice complete, you should be ready and excited for your main event! This is your time to be nimble, flexible, and friendly since you've already prepared as much as you could in advance. Here are a few more principles and practices to keep in mind as you actually deliver the webinar itself.

- **Check in with your audience.** Presenting online can be disorienting for presenters because they often can't see their audience. Ask for audience members to give you a "thumbs up" at times or a quick "OK" message in the chat.

- **Ensure that you have live captions or a live transcript available.** If you can be proactive in encouraging webinar participants to have the tools that they may need to be successful, that's a solid strategy for making your webinar more inclusive.

- **Do not rely on the slide deck for notes.** Put notes in another application (maybe even on your mobile phone or a sheet of paper in front of you!) so you're not tempted to overwhelm the slides.

- **Verbally describe images or diagrams in your slide deck for accessibility purposes.** Offer quick and short descriptions of the visuals you're showing on-screen. For example, if you're showing an image of an open road, weave your description into your narration: "Learning about a new career path is a lot like navigating an open road, kind of like the image I have up on-screen now of a long, curving, one-lane road in the middle of a wooded forest."

- **Use the back channel.** Bring questions over from the chat into your main presentation so that you're letting the live observations you're noticing get a moment in the spotlight.

- **Make people feel seen.** Naming folks who are in the room and offering validation and appreciation for their contributions can really make participants feel like they're part of the experience, not just spectators.

The webinar will likely not go as you expect, so be open to changes. They'll make the webinar better for everyone!

After the Webinar Is Over

Phew, you made it! Once the webinar is over, the bulk of the work is done. However, there are still a couple of follow-up steps you may want to pursue to ensure that the webinar participants had a positive experience and you're getting information that you need to create another successful webinar in the future.

First, share your slide deck after the live event is over. While it's the goal for learners to be engaged during a live presentation, they may not always be able to focus fully and completely during the live presentation time. If the live event conversation doesn't include sensitive dialogue or conversation with learners, you may consider recording the entire multimedia presentation so that you can also share the live recording after the fact.

After you've shared your materials, consider following up with a poll or survey about the live event to gather data for improvement. Ideally, you would even want to have a survey or poll queued up to send right after the event ends so that participants can respond while the webinar is still fresh on their minds. Sending a poll or a survey to your participants signals that you'd value hearing from them in the future. You might also include any "bonus" links, resources, or articles that they may find helpful for continuing the conversation from the webinar. Consider any kind of self-promotion resources as well, such as social media handles for yourself or for the organization that's sponsoring the event.

Give yourself some grace after you've finished a webinar. You'll have done a lot of work to deliver and facilitate communication across multiple channels, from a slide deck to participant engagement tools. But this kind of work should pay off, especially when it comes to building a learner community. We'll return to ways to build a community beyond a live webinar experience in Chapter 9, "Building Connections Among Learners," but for now, recognize that the preparation and work you've done to create an interactive webinar should lay important groundwork for helping learners remember that learning is a social experience, one that requires trust and community building, to be successful.

Takeaways

- **A good webinar should be interactive.** Don't just deliver content; recognize the real people in the room.

- **Create materials that guide participants through an experience.** This webinar is not just about delivering content. Be explicit about what you want them to be able to do during the webinar itself.

- **Practice, practice, practice.** The more comfortable that you feel with the webinar tool and your materials, the more prepared you'll be to engage responsively with live people when they're in the webinar room with you.

- **Make options available for participants during the live webinar.** Give them choices for where, how, and why they can engage. If you respect their needs as participants, they'll respect your needs as a facilitator.

Building Connections Among Learners

A sense of belonging is an essential ingredient of a successful online learning experience. Learning designer Tharon Howard describes this in terms of "social presence," a feeling of belonging, identifying with the community, and sharing a bond with other members of the community.[1] Sadly, many online learning experiences lack this feeling of social presence. Without it, learners quickly disengage and disconnect from the experience.

The more that you can build emotional connections among learners, the better. That's because emotions are one of the most powerful tools you have as a learning designer. Research in learning science has begun to recognize that cognition and emotion are deeply intertwined. As educator and psychologist Sarah Rose Cavanagh writes, "Emotion is already present in all of experiences, perhaps even *particularly* so in cognition."[2] The more strongly you care about something, the more deeply you'll think about it, and the more you'll learn.

Building a learning community is a multilayered process. It takes time to create authentic connections among learners. Superficial attempts to force a community into being usually backfire because there is no "one size fits all" approach for building a community. Think about how a group of working professionals taking a course outside of work may simply want to dip into a discussion forum occasionally to ask questions, while a nurse taking a course for continuing ed certification may prefer a regularly scheduled webinar check-in or a live lunchtime Q&A space. All of that being said, there is one factor in common for all effective communities: being responsive to the community's needs and adapting accordingly. If you can be responsive and engaged with the learners who are in your particular learning context, you can begin the process of creating a community with much greater efficacy.

Bringing Learners Together

To establish a learning community successfully, learning designers have to set the groundwork for a trusting and caring community. That means kicking off the course with activities and conversation starters that help learners actually get to know each other and engage with

---

1   Tharon Howard, *Design to Thrive: Creating Social Networks and Online Communities That Last* (Burlington, MA: Elsevier, 2010), 130.

2   Sarah Rose Cavanagh, *The Spark of Learning: Energizing the College Classroom with the Science of Emotion* (Morganton, WV: West Virginia University Press, 2016), 24.

one another. Importantly, it also means the designer has to think about their own role in the community, too, which requires some keen social awareness and a willingness to be flexible about how different groups of people interact. Even if the learners don't become best friends, they will at least begin to see each other as humans on the other side of the screen, which is essential to building understanding, compassion, and grace in an online learning experience.

Make a Good First Impression

The first experiences that a learner has in a class can make or break their impression of the entire course. Starting off the course with a friendly, welcoming tone and opportunities for learners to share who they are right from the start is a good start toward building some community connection.

Educator Michelle Pacansky-Brock describes how one way to "humanize" online learning is to create a welcome video from the instructor's perspective. A welcome video could be informal; perhaps the designer or the instructor for the course simply records a quick message on their phone or through a webcam to introduce themselves and the course. The welcome video could also be a simple slideshow video created in PowerPoint or a tool like Adobe Express that includes a few pieces of key information about what to expect in the class and what the purpose of the class is.

Even if the learning experience you're designing is not being facilitated by any one particular person, having someone be the name and face of the course can help learners recognize that they're not just taking the course from a robot or a cold, disengaged presence, but from someone who actually cares.

Build "Meet-and-Greet" Spaces

It's a good idea to offer learners in your class the opportunity to share a little about themselves at the start of the learning experience. A popular method for doing this is creating a discussion forum where participants can write a quick post sharing a few sentences about who they are and what they're hoping to get out of the class. Simply creating space for individual learners to share their lives can set the tone to demonstrate that individuals will be seen and appreciated in the class.

Figure 9.1 shows a script from a welcome video (just over one minute long!) that Jenae made for a college writing and speaking class. In this video, she gives a very brief overview of what learners will do in the class and how the class might be different from others they've taken before. She doesn't say much about herself (other welcome videos may include more information about the instructor), but she offers an invitation to support the students in the ongoing work that they may be doing.

Script:

> "Hi, everyone! Welcome to our class. I'm Jenae, I'm your instructor. This is just a quick overview of what to expect from the quarter. We're going to start the quarter developing your own research idea and then you're going to spend the rest of the quarter conducting that research, trying to answer a research question that interests you. And then, you'll get to present that research as a new expert. So, basically, what's different than previous writing courses you might have taken is that you start with one idea, you pursue that in one big project over the course of the whole quarter, but you present that project in multiple modes, meaning that you write about it, you present about it, and you create multimedia about it. You'll get a lot of support in this class, both from your peers and from me. Basically, we're going to be a collaborative research community, and we're going to work together to ensure that you're thinking a lot about the best ways and the best modes for communicating your ideas. I'm excited to work with you this quarter and can't wait for all of the awesome research projects we're going to get to explore. Don't hesitate to reach out to me if you have any questions or you want to follow up on any of this."

FIGURE 9.1
This Welcome video in Jenae's class includes a clear image of Jenae and a student working together to illustrate the conversational and collaborative nature of the class community.

You can also give individuals options: They could create their own video and post it, or simply share a photo of themselves. Some of these choices can help learners feel like they have some choice in how they want to present themselves and be part of the community.

Meet-and-greet spaces can also be responsive to more specific prompts or activities. For example, you could create a Google map or some other kind of virtual map and ask learners to put a "pin" in the map to identify where in the world they're joining the course from (see Figure 9.2). This idea can be a good way to kick off conversations about where people in the course live and show learners that there are other people like them all around the world who are engaging in the same experience.

FIGURE 9.2
Learners can pin their locations on a shared Google map to show where they're living and engaging in the class community.

You could also design an activity where learners annotate a document or an image relevant to the course together. For example, if you are facilitating a course about data analytics, you might find a data visualization to look at together that could kick off some dialogue about what learners in the class notice about the data visualization. Starting off with a shared space for everyone to comment on can help learners find some areas of common connection or shared interest.

Create a Safe and Brave Environment

From the beginning, it's important for you to work with the learners in your community to develop social norms so that the learning environment feels safe for everyone. Marginalized members of your learning community, from people of color to women and LGBTQ+-identified individuals, to learners from multiracial or multilingual backgrounds, may not feel welcome in your learning environment by default. To create a truly inclusive environment and build a welcoming community, acknowledge and appreciate what members of marginalized communities will bring to your particular learning space. Importantly, empower those learners to be agential and active members of the community.

Include a policy in your welcome video or in a welcome forum where you state explicitly that bullying or discriminatory behavior will not be tolerated. Be specific about a zero-tolerance policy for hostile language (including use of racial, ableist, or sexist slurs), which includes a ban on linking to inappropriate images or videos in the course. Name the consequences for engaging in these behaviors: any learner who engages in hostile or discriminatory behavior will be removed from the class. Practices like moderating comments before they are posted may need to be named as a consequence that could go into effect if discriminatory behavior is witnessed.

Beyond establishing a basic zero-tolerance, anti-harassment policy, a safe learning environment can also be cultivated by establishing collaborative community norms. Invite learners in the class to submit, via an anonymous forum, a suggestion or two for what kinds of behaviors they'd like to see from their peers and from you in order to feel like they can share and engage safely in the learning community. You can invite learners to share more than a sentence or two if they would like, but requesting even just one idea from each member of the learning community can all be part of a shared document with the list of suggestions for the whole learning community to refer to when they are asked to interact and engage with each other.

If you find that some of the suggestions in the community norms activity are in conflict, don't panic! As the facilitator, you will need to make some executive decisions about conflicting norms and acknowledge that you made that choice to the learning community, once you have shared the results. So, as the facilitator, you must develop a clear understanding for yourself about what you would expect to see from a learning community. You may need to revisit these norms and approach them flexibly if they are not working.

Always have a space somewhere in your course website for learners to submit feedback about concerns they are having. It is all too easy for the most marginalized members of a learning community to get lost or have concerns that are unmet. Actively invite input and feedback throughout the learning experience to ensure that the course itself is not causing anyone harm. Just be sure to respond if you're receiving input; too many students have the experience of giving extensive feedback, only to receive no response in kind and to feel like they've poured their hearts into a black box. Even a short response thanking and acknowledging the suggestions will go a long way toward empowering learners to have an authentic voice in their experience. As you receive suggestions on how the course is going, you also have an opportunity to go back, revise the class norms, and create ground rules for conduct that respect and give everyone an equal opportunity to succeed and engage.

Take the Temperature

Helping learners see *why* they are in the class experience together can help learners create some connections to others from the very beginning of the course experience. In a writing class that Jenae taught, she asked students to take a survey at the start of the term to assess experiences with their own writing. The survey was simple: a lot of "true" or "false" questions about prior experiences with being in writing classes, as shown in Figure 9.3.

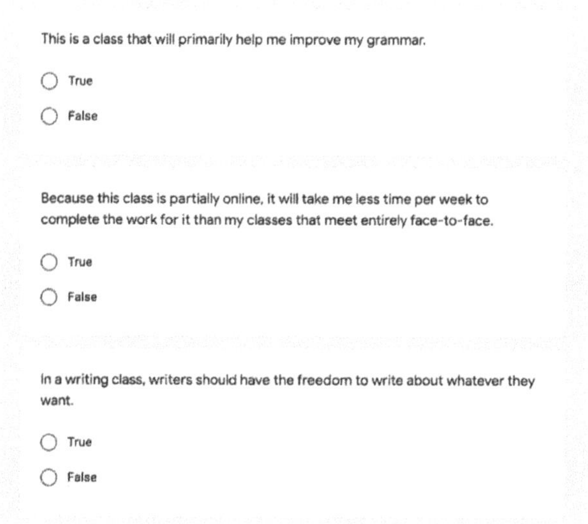

This is a class that will primarily help me improve my grammar.

○ True

○ False

Because this class is partially online, it will take me less time per week to complete the work for it than my classes that meet entirely face-to-face.

○ True

○ False

In a writing class, writers should have the freedom to write about whatever they want.

○ True

○ False

FIGURE 9.3
Jenae distributes an anonymous survey in her writing classes to get a sense of how students' attitudes about the class (and their experiences as writers) differ and overlap.

After a quorum of learners completed the survey, Jenae published the anonymized results so that everyone could see them. The results were often varied and surprising; much of the time, the group generally didn't think that they'd be improving their grammar in a writing class, but they were more split on whether writers should have freedom to write about whatever they wanted. Jenae found it important to talk through the results of the survey, so she would often record a short video summarizing the results, weaving in reflection with even more detail about what to expect from the class experience beyond her welcome video. This approach was her way of being responsive to the class's experience and pointing out areas of shared perspective and areas of difference.

She then also created a discussion board where members of the class could share what surprised them about their shared or differing expectations. This discussion gave learners an opportunity to chime in beyond the anonymous survey result if they wanted to speak more to their experiences or responses on the survey.

These kinds of surveys are basically a way to "take the temperature" in a class environment: they are easy to complete, don't require much time or investment, and immediately reveal a lot about shared or differing values in a class context. They can be a launching point for further discussion either with the instructor or with peers at any given moment in the course.

If you're facilitating live webinars in the class, surveys can be launched live as a way to gather real-time information about how a certain activity is feeling or how nimbly the group is orienting to a particular set of ideas. But even if you're not facilitating live webinars, surveys can be administered outside of real time and results shared even just a day later, which can generate the same kinds of conversations about how the class is feeling and what their attitudes or perspectives are on any given component of the class experience. "Temperature-taking" surveys are as much of a tool for the facilitator as they are for the rest of the class community.

Building Connections over Time

Being proactive in communicating with learners in your class is critical in an online learning community. When online, it's all too easy for people to feel detached or disconnected, especially if they are not frequently convening in real-time interactions. Your learners are rarely as focused on your course content as you are. They may lose the thread of the course content at any time. In online learning environments, especially, they can get lost or check out for weeks at a time. You can easily lose students entirely if you don't structure occasions for informal and sometimes more formal check-ins with them.

Learners who are marginalized are often less likely to ask for help, and, conversely, learners who have grown up with privilege are often the first to ask for help or lean on instructors or other resources. It's your job to design opportunities to ask your students if they need help. Don't wait until someone fails or disappears entirely.

To build more equity into your course's experience, create a consistent and recognizable pattern for sending check-in emails or announcements. The more structured and recognizable the pattern of your communication with learners is, the better, so that they understand when it is a good time to reach out to you or their peers and ask for help. Send out a check-in message every Monday, for example. It could also mean sending out a check-in message after every major assignment or every main unit in the course. It doesn't really matter what the pattern for your check-in is so long as there is a clear pattern where learners can expect to hear from you in timely and distinct intervals.

Keep your check-ins short and to-the-point. Acknowledge the work that your learners are doing and simply invite them to come to you if they need anything. If you're noticing patterns where learners are getting stuck in the course or having trouble, acknowledge those problem areas in your check-ins, too, and use those as a way to invite further questions or discussion that learners may want to have with you or with each other.

Here's an example of what a full group check-in might look like. This kind of full group check-in message could be sent via email, it could be posted to an Announcements space within a learning management system or course website, or it could be pushed to students via a discussion board designed for course announcements.

"Hi, everyone! Hope you all are having a great week and that this week's activities are going smoothly for you. [**You could write a similar opener where you say something kind of welcoming to demonstrate that you care about student engagement in the course.**] I've noticed that everyone's doing a great job keeping up with the pace of the activities. (I know it's a lot!) [**It's valuable to acknowledge the workload in the class and the impact it may be having on learners.**] If you ever need an extension or an assignment opened back up, please don't hesitate to let me know. Typically, an extension can be accommodated with a short grace period; we just need to stay in touch about it. [**You may not be offering such an extension or "grace period" in your own learning context, but a check-in reminder on some core course policies or participation options may be valuable to provide in a full group check-in since learners may not always remember what is or isn't allowed in the course.**]

I wanted to let you all know that I really enjoyed reading your responses in the latest assignment so far and wanted to offer some feedback based on a few patterns I noticed. [**You might want to write one to two bullet points here about areas of potential confusion or patterns in common mistakes that a lot of learners in the course may be making.**]

Hope this helps! I look forward to being in touch with all of you and continuing to see your excellent work."

If you can, include a short video or voice memo with your check-in, which can be more compelling for your learners if you really want to personalize your check-ins. It can add yet another human touch to your communications.

The check-in should be a simple, but effective, measure for demonstrating to learners that there is a human at the other end of the online learning experience who is thinking of them and wants to acknowledge their work and progress.

The Quick Email Check-In

Consider going beyond the big group check-in to write some individual notes to students in your learning environment. It's easy for learners to gloss over group announcements or mass emails and assume that the message is not for them. But if you write a quick, personalized message to the students in your class, it can make a big difference. And it won't actually take that long to do. It can honestly take one minute (or less!) if you write a short template version of your email that you can then customize with learners' names. You don't have to ask anything specific: just ask your learners how things are going.

For example, you might consider a template like this:

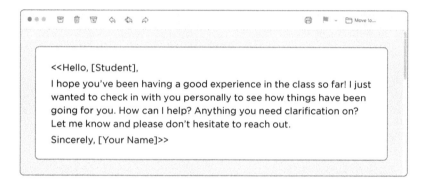

Often, learners will report things they are having trouble with or issues with the course design. It's a fundamental principle of user experience design that you have to ask how your users are doing. Don't assume things are working fine if you don't ask.

If you have students who have been absent or missing work, you may want to compose a slightly more formal email, like this:

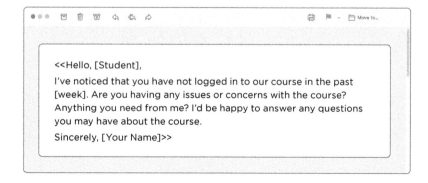

We have seen some amazing results from doing email check-ins like this. Once you start creating these occasions, you will find that many learners will be grateful and may open up about things you may be able to address. And these kinds of check-ins can be sent whether you are meeting with students in real time or even if you are just facilitating the course outside of real time.

If you have designed a course that stays open outside of a particular set course term or time frame and you are simply looking for feedback, build in times when, after completing a certain segment of the course content, an automatic email or survey is sent to the learner to check in. That way, feedback is triggered at a key time in the course and can accomplish two things at once: It can give you, as the facilitator, valuable feedback about how the course is running so far, and it can help demonstrate to the learner that there is, in fact, someone on the other end of the course who is checking in and ensuring the successful completion of the course. Even an automatic push can indicate caring, which is core to community building.

Group Check-Ins

Depending on your comfort level, you may want to encourage group check-ins. These check-ins are often real-time, small group conversations with either the same group of learners on a regular basis or with different cohorts of learners by request. Doing a check-in in real time can reveal concerns or questions that some learners may be reluctant to share alone. One vocal learner may bring questions to the group that would not come up in one-on-one sessions. The power of the group can be persuasive! Often, one person will say something that can speak for the whole group.

This doesn't have to be a time-consuming process to arrange, especially if you have a template invitation at your disposal and you request that the learners sign up for the consults on their own (although, it is a viable alternative to assign small group check-ins and construct the groups in advance as a task). You might consider something like:

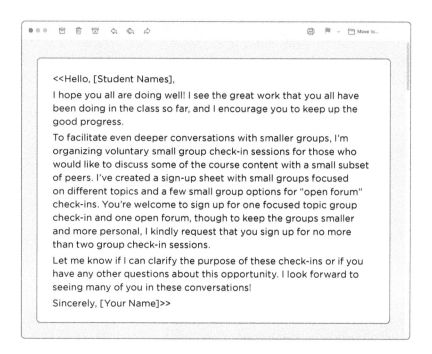

> <<Hello, [Student Names],
>
> I hope you all are doing well! I see the great work that you all have been doing in the class so far, and I encourage you to keep up the good progress.
>
> To facilitate even deeper conversations with smaller groups, I'm organizing voluntary small group check-in sessions for those who would like to discuss some of the course content with a small subset of peers. I've created a sign-up sheet with small groups focused on different topics and a few small group options for "open forum" check-ins. You're welcome to sign up for one focused topic group check-in and one open forum, though to keep the groups smaller and more personal, I kindly request that you sign up for no more than two group check-in sessions.
>
> Let me know if I can clarify the purpose of these check-ins or if you have any other questions about this opportunity. I look forward to seeing many of you in these conversations!
>
> Sincerely, [Your Name]>>

Arranging these group check-ins may be logistically quite challenging if you are facilitating a course that doesn't meet in real time or that has a large number of learners involved. But if you have the capacity, a conversation with a smaller group can bring out interesting ideas and questions that may not have come out in a larger group setting.

Bring Your World to Others

Even with webinars, online discussions, and email check-ins, it can be easy to lose sight of the fact that there are real people behind the computer screens. Designing activities where members of the learning community can bring their outside selves into the class can help remind learners of the fuller life experiences that the learners within the class community might have.

As an activity, you might ask learners to go offline for a component of an activity and then report back with documentation of that activity. It might mean asking learners to take photos of something in their neighborhood, hometown, or even just around their house. With some instructions on how to upload the photos they take and share them within the online portal, learners have an opportunity to bring some of their offline lives into their online learning experience.

For example, in a training on accessible design, a designer might create an activity where the online learners are asked to take a walk in their neighborhood or around their office and find one or two examples of accommodations or accessible design in architecture (see Figure 9.4). The learners might be asked to take a picture of what the architectural design or accommodation looks like and post those pictures to a shared discussion forum or perhaps a collaborative document, like a "Wiki"-style page where the class could share a compendium of examples together. That way, learners can see many examples of accessible design from locations around the world! For example, some learners might find pictures of wheelchair accessible ramps while others might locate Braille on elevators. Still others might analyze how height-adjustable chairs or sit/stand desks offer accommodations for different kinds of bodies.

| Laptop Stand | SR/Stand Desk | Automatic Water Dispenser | Book Holder | Building Ramp Next to Stairs | Moveable Carts |

FIGURE 9.4

A collaborative digital pinboard space, such as Padlet, Microsoft Whiteboard, or Google Jamboard, can be used for different students to post pictures or illustrations of ideas in response to a shared prompt. Here is an example from Padlet of pictures of accessible design in different places.

These kinds of "scavenger hunt" activities where learners are invited to bring something from their offline worlds into the online learning space can make learners feel like the online experience is not just an impersonal and disconnected experience from their real lives, but rather that their online and offline selves and spaces can be merged and brought together.

When Things Go Wrong

Inevitably, creating connections between people can sometimes cause conflicts or challenges. The more that learners reveal about themselves to others, the more opportunities there are for implicit biases and discrimination to crop up and impact the interaction. Learners from marginalized backgrounds are commonly targets of online discrimination and bullying, and this isn't any less true in a learning context.

You might have already established some norms to create a safe and inclusive learning environment, but simply establishing norms may not be enough to prevent a sexist, ableist, ageist, or otherwise discriminatory social interaction from happening in your course. If you witness any kind of bullying or harmful interaction as a facilitator, it is your responsibility to intervene and discuss the interaction with all parties involved in the interaction.

If the negative social interaction happened in real time during a class webinar, de-escalate the situation in real time. As a facilitator, don't ignore the harm done; instead, address it and move on. For example, you could say something out loud like, "Jason, let's remember our community norms and focus on cultivating respect for our peers." You could even put a link into the webinar chat for the community norms if you see that a member of the class community is in violation of those norms. Consider sending a private chat message, if possible, to the perpetrator of the harmful comment requesting that you speak with them more after the formal session is over on the phone or via email. You might also want to send a note to the person who received the harmful comment and ask if you can do anything to support them or if they would like to talk with you one-on-one.

In a live moment, things can get heated, so it may be challenging both for the perpetrator of the harmful comment or the recipient of the harmful comment to respond. If the harmful interaction happened in real time, be sure to follow-up outside of real time. A brief email would suffice with a simple check-in:

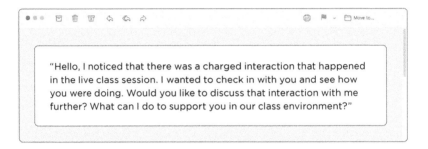

"Hello, I noticed that there was a charged interaction that happened in the live class session. I wanted to check in with you and see how you were doing. Would you like to discuss that interaction with me further? What can I do to support you in our class environment?"

Asking how both learners are doing, whether they perpetuated the harm or were on the receiving end of the harm, indicates that you are there to support all of the students in the class environment and that you are willing to extend empathy to the learners in the class without necessarily excusing or condoning harmful behavior.

If a harmful interaction happens outside of a real-time interaction, such as in a hateful discussion forum post or in a link to an image or video-based content that's shared with the class that's offensive, leave a comment directly in the discussion board that addresses the comment, pointing the class again to the community norms. If there is a racial slur or hateful language or imagery in anything posted in a formal class space, it is within your right to remove or delete that content so that it does not continue to perpetuate harm.

Reach out via email or a direct message to the person who posted the harmful comment and explain your reasoning, particularly if you needed to remove content that they posted. You might also send a separate message to the entire class community, addressing the incident (without directly naming the poster of the content), acknowledging any pain or hurt that might have been experienced. Again, when harmful interactions happen, it is much better to address the harm caused than it is to ignore it or pretend it didn't happen, even if it feels uncomfortable to do so.

Keeping Communities Strong

To keep your online communities strong, maintain three core principles: being flexible, responsive, and timely. These three principles are intended to help you have more successful interactions with the learners in your class so that your communication remains strong and that you're bringing real human presence to the class. Practicing all of these principles at the same time may not always be possible. Give yourself grace if you can't always be as flexible as you need to be as the instructor. However, when there are opportunities to be open to responsiveness to your class environment, the better the experience will likely be for everyone.

Flexible

In a formal learning environment, a lot of the community-building interactions may happen in a given space or time. However, in an online learning environment, learners can reach you and each other at any given time any day of the week. The fact is that individuals take online classes so that they have flexibility to engage with and complete the content at times when it's convenient to them. Your students' times for course completion and engagement may not always align with your own availability or your ideal schedule though. As the facilitator, you may want to set expectations about your own response time to messages so that students know you're present but they won't have the expectation that you'll respond within minutes of their own response. For example, you might be clear that you respond to messages within 24 hours of receiving them.

You don't have to bend over backward to accommodate other people's schedules. However, you might consider periodically checking in on your online learning experience at shorter intervals over the course of a full seven-day week instead of limiting your time in the course to traditional "business hours," Monday–Friday. If you don't have the capacity to do that, it's OK. But if you can manage your own time flexibly and create varied, short check-in points for the course rather than blocking large, concentrated chunks of time to respond to or work on the course, you may find that you catch more engagements that may be happening around the clock and that you can be responsive to different groups of individual learners than if you only worked on the course at the same time every day.

Responsive

To create a genuinely user-centered learning experience, you need to be responsive to the learners in the online learning environment. That means taking the feedback you see from learners and responding to it within a reasonable time frame. This can be time-consuming, but it is critical for building trust and cultivating the kind of community that will make your learning experience more effective.

Unexpected interactions will likely happen in an online learning environment, too. Accept that those will happen with an open mind and prepare to change your plans once you see what the learners in your particular course are responding to or appreciating. You may not be able to change fundamental parts of the course in response to the learners that are in it, but you can make small tweaks that demonstrate a willingness to think flexibly in response to what you're seeing, hearing, and experiencing from learners in the course.

Timely

Things happen quickly online. Learners in an online class are going to have expectations for faster response rates to work that they've submitted or comments they've received than if they were attending a learning experience in an on-site location. Create very clear expectations very early on about how quickly you, as the facilitator, will respond to assignments and feedback so that learners don't feel concerned if they are not getting the kinds of immediate responses they may expect from learning in an online environment.

If you are not seeing a community formed right away, be patient. Building trust and connection can take a lot of time, and there may be learners in your learning environment who just aren't as invested or engaged as others. A learner's lack of engagement does not necessarily mean that you have done a poor job of building a user-centered experience. Rather, recognize that not all users will be universally served by the kind of class you are designing. The best you can do is anticipate, to the extent that you can, what most learners will value and design based on what you know about the people who are in your learning environment.

Remember that creating a class community often requires a special mix of having the right people gathered in the right place at the right times who are all willingly and fully invested in learning together. As the facilitator, be kind to yourself and be compassionate about the work that you are doing. You can only do so much, and trust that if you come into the work with a caring mindset, you will create a meaningful learning environment.

Takeaways

- **Start off warm and personal.** An early, welcoming invitation to get to know you and the other learners in the class will move the learning experience in a collegial direction.

- **Pace yourself.** Don't start off highly engaged as the facilitator and then burn out and never touch base. Create email templates in advance that you can send on a set schedule throughout the learning experience to demonstrate your investment in your learner's journey through the course from start to finish. You don't have to do all of your communications all at once. Set some boundaries and expectations as you go.

- **Create a safe environment.** It is important to ensure that all learners feel safe enough to learn effectively. Create norms that establish ethical, respectable conduct among peers in the class community.

- **Think outside the box.** Creating community doesn't just happen with real-time conversation. Create activities where learners can share more about their homes, their hobbies, their families, and their interests.

- **Be flexible.** When you're working and responding with real people, things will never go quite as you expect. Embrace the change and have fun connecting with other humans!

Giving Your Learners Feedback

Most learners are largely motivated by the end result of their course: to feel more successful, make more money, gain more recognition, or simply feel like they can improve their own or their families' lives through their education. Failing to achieve these goals can feel immensely personal in large part because the goals for learning *are* deeply personal. Even earning one negative grade or one negative evaluation on a component of a course that is part of their larger journey to completion can scare people into thinking that they may never achieve the end goal that they may so desire.

Students shouldn't feel scared to receive feedback, however. A critical part of learning is knowing when you understand the material and when you need more information. The sooner and more frequently learners can get feedback that's supportive or low stakes, the less unnerving it will feel. Providing feedback early and often loops all the way back to our discussion in Chapter 3, "Setting the Foundation," about learning goals: When learners know how well they're doing, they have the chance to see whether they're meeting the learning goals or not.

There's a lot of unfulfilled promises in the world of online learning for giving learners continuous and frequent feedback about how well they're understanding the course content. Often, this promise is not fulfilled because it is a lot of work for a designer and a facilitator to be immediately responsive to learners throughout a course. Time constraints are a real concern, but there are some ways to leverage low-touch, automated feedback that can have a big impact. Personalized feedback doesn't have to be time-consuming, and it can ultimately make a lot of difference for the student's experience.

Our philosophy is that we love to design learning experiences that everyone can succeed in. To create a truly user-centered experience, we think first about how learners will know whether they're succeeding and what it will look like for them to recognize when they are actually learning.

> **NOTE** FEEDBACK FOR THE CLASS VS. FEEDBACK FOR YOU
>
> Chapter 11, "Reviewing Your Learning Experience," explores how to *get* useful feedback on your learning experience, from learners and from yourself. It also focuses on reflection and lessons learned after your course is over. In contrast, this chapter is concerned with how to *give* useful, actionable feedback to learners.

Creating the Stakes

As a learning designer, you have to make some careful choices about how learners can assess their success within a course. A lot of online courses lean heavily on multiple-choice quizzes as the primary way for learners to get feedback. Multiple-choice quizzes are easy both for the learners to take and for the designers to create. For the learners, they do not have to write or independently conjure up any ideas; they just have to select from a list of options and, upon submission of their quiz, they receive immediate feedback about which questions they answered correctly. For designers, multiple-choice quizzes are very useful for designing quick knowledge checks for learners; as a designer, you can quickly see how many questions the learners answered correctly and can create some clear metrics for common patterns in questions that are frequently answered incorrectly.

But if you want to assess a learner's ability to do something or think critically about a topic, a multiple-choice quiz isn't going to work. This isn't to say that a multiple-choice quiz can't be challenging, but the focus of a multiple-choice quiz is on the learner's understanding of content, not on the learner's understanding of how to apply the content to a variety of different contexts.

Let's say that you're designing an online project management course. By the end of the course, your learners should be able to understand some basic principles of project management so that they can create better project timelines and allocate project resources appropriately. While there may be some inherently wrong approaches to project management that could be assessed in a multiple-choice quiz, a skilled project manager is likely not going to be dealing with obvious "right" and "wrong" ways to manage a project. Most projects require complex interactions with people. As such, there may be multiple decisions a project manager needs to make and, within the scope of an online course, it could be really hard to identify what skills a budding project manager needs to develop through multiple-choice quizzes alone.

So, what kinds of assessments could you use beyond multiple-choice quizzes and when should you use them? There's a lot of complexity to these choices and, as a designer, you ultimately need to align what you want people in the course to learn with how you think they can best demonstrate evidence of that learning. But there are a few common reasons that designers may choose to implement certain kinds of assessment instruments, as shown in Table 10.1.

TABLE 10.1 CHOOSING YOUR ASSESSMENT

Assessment Instrument	When to Use It
Multiple-Choice Quiz or Exam	To assess a learner's understanding of a concept, definition, or specific process. Could also be used to assess responses or reactions to a scenario-based question if there are clear "right" or "wrong" responses.
Open-Ended Questions	To assess a learner's ability to interpret and apply a new idea. Could also be used to assess a learner's ability to describe an approach to a process or problem.
Long-Form Written Assignment (for example, a research paper, a white paper, or a memo)	To assess a learner's ability to make an argument, analyze a text or current event, or use outside evidence to inform a particular claim. Could also be used to assess a learner's understanding of how to produce a piece of writing specific to a particular field or discipline (for example, a lab report in a lab sciences context or a policy memo in a public policy context).
Project (for example, building a database, creating a website, or creating a video or podcast, etc.)	To assess a learner's ability to make a new product and apply skills learned to build an independent project. Could also be used to assess a learner's understanding of how to create a field-specific artifact (for example, a data dashboard in a data analytics course).
Portfolio (for example, a collection of work that a learner has completed over a period of time)	To assess a learner's ability to grow, revise, and create a body of work over a particular period of time. Could also be used to assess a learner's readiness to enter into a professional field where portfolios are required to determine experience (for example, an architecture portfolio for a career in building design or a social media portfolio for a career in social media marketing).

A lot of learning experiences will implement a combination of these types of assessments in their final course, and it's likely that at different phases of your course and for different purposes, you will need to select more than one assessment or evaluation method. Remember that an assessment serves two purposes: It helps the learners recognize where they are in the course so that they have an understanding of the progress, and it helps you, as the facilitator, see what challenges and triumphs the learners are experiencing all the way throughout the course.

DON'T SWEAT CHEATING

A lot of learning designers may be concerned about learners "cheating" on built-in exams or quizzes, and they will try to block learners from opening separate windows or tabs while finishing a quiz. However, most learners on the web tend to do research to get answers while they're online; it feels unnatural and counter to the design of being online not to look something up in a separate window while engaging in another one. With the rise in AI-assisted writing technology, such as ChatGPT, learners may even start to become more acclimated to using outside assistance in generating new ideas for their writing with AI assistance.

Rather than feeling concerned about cheating, consider ways to write quiz or assignment questions that *use* the learners' abilities to access the web so they can apply the answers they might find across the web to demonstrate their understanding of a concept rather than simply finding information on the web to regurgitate memorized facts. Similarly, in the case of assignments that ask students to write, think about how they can work with AI assistance to generate ideas rather than trying to "ban" or forbid usage of such tools. While there may be some cases where the goal of the course is for a learner to memorize a particular term, concept, or policy, it is more likely that learners will remember the information better if they have to apply a term, concept, policy, or any other fact that they can look up from the course to a particular situation or problem. Similarly, with writing, a better assignment might ask students to integrate multiple perspectives into their response, using ChatGPT to help them generate initial ideas, while asking students to consider how other source material or ideas may inform what a tool like ChatGPT may produce.

Quality or Quantity

When it comes to designing your learning experience, you'll need to consider a core question: Is it meaningful to give learners feedback based on the quality of their submissions or responses? Or is simply checking their work for completion enough to demonstrate achievement of the course's outcomes?

How you give learners feedback depends on the contexts, goals, and outcomes for the course. If you are designing a one-off training or workshop experience where it's most important simply to show evidence of skills gained, then grading for completion is likely enough. But if you are designing a full course sequence that supports the completion of a certificate or degree program, then grading for quality may be worthwhile, especially if the value of the certificate or degree depends upon the production and completion of high-quality work.

There may be some learning contexts where it is challenging to assess the quality of the work. In a class on meditation, for example, there may not be one "right" way to assess a learner's ability to meditate successfully since the process of meditation is deeply personal and variable. In that situation, simply verifying that the learner has, in fact, engaged in a meditation practice regularly and been actively part of group conversations about the challenges (and benefits) of meditation may be enough to merit their good work and completion of the course criteria.

When you're making decisions about how to assess learning in your experience, consider asking yourself the following questions:

- To what extent can the quality of work submitted for this course be reasonably assessed?
- How much does it matter that this course distinguishes between low- or high-quality work?
- How important is the production of "high-quality" work for maintaining the value of the learning experience being designed?

These questions are a starting point rather than an ending point, but they may help you calibrate your thinking if you're feeling on the fence about the best way to approach assessing students' work in your course.

Give Learners Choices

Whenever you have the opportunity to give learners a choice about how they are assessed in their course, do so, because it's better. This is not always possible, especially with a large class. However, if learners can have a choice about whether to receive, say, written or voice-recorded feedback, or whether they would like to receive a numerical score or not, these choices help the students feel empowered over how they can improve and respond to critical feedback.

There are several circumstances in which giving students an option for how they receive feedback can be useful. You could give learners a choice about what kind of feedback to receive if the following situations are relevant:

- **The way that learners complete the assessment is not that important.** If you just want the learner to come to the "right" answer in some way or there are multiple "right" ways to express an idea, then there is no downside to a choice for assessment.

- **You (or the course facilitator) have the capacity to give feedback on different kinds of submissions.** If a human is involved in the course regularly and actively and has the capacity to respond just as easily to a piece of writing as to, say, a voice memo, then it's better for the learners to have that choice.

- **The learning management system or course design software you're using can accept multiple submission types.** Be sure that you're aware of all the limitations or affordances in your course management application before making choices available.

Assuming that these conditions are met, you'll then want to think about what kinds of choices are possible for the types of assessments you might be designing. There are a number of good options to consider here, although whether these options seem appropriate will depend on your ability to align the assessment with the goal and activities that learners are engaging in throughout your course (see Table 10.2).

TABLE 10.2 FLEXIBLE OPTIONS FOR COMPLETING ASSESSMENTS

Assessment Instrument	Ways That Students Can Complete the Assessment
Open-Ended Questions	In writing or through voice memo/audio clip.
Long-Form Written Assignment (a research paper, a white paper, or a memo)	In writing or through voice memo/audio clip.
Project (building a database, creating a website, creating a video or podcast, etc.)	In writing, in an illustration/graphic, in voice memo/audio clip, in a video, in a spreadsheet, in a PowerPoint presentation. The options here are basically endless and will depend on the scope of the project.
Portfolio (a collection of work that a learner has completed over a period of time)	A website, a collection of documents in a folder, or a video.

Giving a learner even just one alternate way to complete an assessment can make them feel like they have more agency in the learning experience and that they are completing the assessment in a way that enables them to use their strengths. Better yet, creating at least one additional option can also make a course more accessible. You may have students that are using assistive technologies that could make some forms of response (for example, writing) more difficult for them than other forms of response (for example, speaking). The more you can anticipate choices to help students participate and engage more easily, the better.

When to Use Automated Feedback

A lot of learning experiences will have high enrollments, and it simply will not be possible for a facilitator to craft individualized feedback for every single learner. You may need to use automated feedback in situations like the following:

- **Grading multiple-choice quizzes or exams:** Most quiz and exam creation tools should allow you to indicate which responses are right and wrong so that learners can get immediate feedback on their performance without having to wait for a human to manually score the answers.

- **In explaining the "right" or "wrong" answers:** In many quiz and exam design tools, an explanation for a "right" or "wrong" answer can be displayed as soon as the learner has received their automated score. That way, the learner gets some written feedback on why their response was correct or incorrect.

- **In marking assignments for completion:** Most learning management or course design systems can automatically give learners scores for completion upon assignment submission.

- **In giving general advice and feedback on short answer responses:** Just as in the situation where you can preprogram explanations for "right" or "wrong" answers for a multiple-choice quiz, you could similarly preprogram feedback for short answer responses that explain why a particular short answer is correct or incorrect. This will only work if you are asking for a one- or two-word response.

In these situations, learners will likely not notice or care if a person is not giving them a personalized response. Automated assessments can free up facilitator time to offer feedback and build connections in contexts for the course beyond the assessments themselves. For example, if a facilitator has implemented automated feedback, they can spend more time in the course sending out group check-in announcements or getting involved in responding to low-stakes discussion board responses to create an instructor presence without having to write out individualized comments and feedback. That said, some learners may desire some human feedback on the quality of their submission, even if it doesn't really matter what the quality is like for the sake of completing the course. If, as a facilitator, you have the capacity to give learners the option to receive feedback upon request, you could consider creating a survey or request form for learners to ask for personalized feedback on particular submissions.

The largest cost for implementing automated assessments is in driving students' motivation. Social interactions and connection can often compel learners better than almost anything else. When learners know that there isn't a person actually reading or scoring their work, they might feel like no one else is invested in their experience except for themselves. Students who are more motivated by social interaction may need more of a "push" from someone in the learning community to help them. This is where some of the community-building techniques discussed in Chapter 9, "Building Connections Among Learners," may come into play.

As a designer, you're ultimately making a judgment call for what your learners will need based on the circumstances of the particular course you're working on. Most designers are constrained by lack of time and sufficient resources to build the perfect course. Using automated feedback can be a welcome relief and, again, in many cases, can be both appropriate and sufficient for learners.

When to Ask Learners to Assess Themselves

A powerful and underrated way to give students feedback is to flip the script: ask learners to self-assess! It can be quite powerful for a student to articulate their perception of their performance or understanding and to use that self-reflection to propel their own growth.

Learner self-assessment is most effective in a few particular situations:

- In engaging with highly personal or sensitive content
- In working in a content area that doesn't have a clear "right" or "wrong" answer
- In practicing a particular skill that requires the development of a repetitive habit or routine (for example, exercising, developing a writing practice, etc.)

Asking learners to self-assess can open up different and very powerful ways to provide feedback as a facilitator. Facilitators might be able to, for example, skim through the student self-assessments, see where the patterns are, and share what they're noticing about those patterns with the class community (while keeping personal responses anonymous to protect privacy). That kind of feedback can demonstrate that there is still a human involved in the course without the facilitator needing to spend a lot of time writing individualized feedback for each and every learner in the class who is engaging in the self-assessment.

When and How to Craft Individualized Feedback

If you've decided that the quality of the students' work is the most important thing to assess in order to achieve a course outcome, then taking the time to craft individualized feedback for learners will contribute to greater odds of their success. This is particularly true if you are designing a course that has been advertised as personalized and that is small enough to create a personal atmosphere. Refusing to fulfill this expectation could create learner resentment and confusion.

Even if your class is large, you may still want to consider incorporating individualized student feedback into your course if you've chosen to design an assignment that is large, high-stakes, and has multiple parts to complete, such as a project or a portfolio. For multipart projects or portfolios, the success of the final product is dependent on the completion of drafts or stages of the project prior to its completion. As such, giving individualized feedback on each part will allow students to have greater odds of completing the final project successfully.

However, giving individualized feedback can be an incredibly time-consuming task for a facilitator. It's easy to go overboard with giving written or audio feedback to learners, and many educators lament the amount of time it takes to "grade" student work. If you need to give individualized feedback, maximize the utility of the feedback you're giving while resisting the easy temptation to go "overboard."

Read or Skim the Submission Before Responding

Whether the student has submitted a project, a written assignment, a video, or a spreadsheet, take just three minutes to look at the work without writing down any notes or responding in any way. Gauge what your initial reaction is to the work: What do you notice? What is happening in the student's work? Then jot down a bullet-point list of your observations—not your judgments or critiques—to help guide the feedback you'll give. If you jump to criticism or judgment right away, you will likely waste time questioning or criticizing something that could get corrected later in the piece or submission. If you get a feel for the overall submission first and then craft your suggestions and areas for improvement based on your observations, you'll have spent more time targeting the most important areas in need of feedback.

Identify Two to Three Areas for Improvement

It's hard for learners to process a lot of feedback. Research also shows that most students don't read all of the feedback they're given if they're given too much information to process. As a responder, try to make your feedback really concrete and limit the amount of feedback you have for the learner in just two to three bullet points. Your two to three bullet point areas could speak to trends that you notice in the student's work or could simply be two to three priorities that the student needs to improve or consider in order for their work to be of the highest quality possible.

Importantly, when prioritizing the two to three areas in need of feedback, don't get hung up on mechanical errors or "typos." These kinds of errors are easy for learners to catch on their own or with spell-check software. In most learning situations, perfection is usually not the goal of the assessment anyway. What you're primarily looking for is a demonstration that a student has learned, processed, or understood something new for the first time. The more meaningful feedback will be about "big-picture" concerns and their thinking, not about overall "polish" of the work itself.

Consider Giving Audio or Video Feedback

Recording yourself giving feedback in an audio memo or a short video can be faster than giving written feedback. For students, too, listening to the feedback could be a more beneficial experience than reading a bunch of detailed notes. Listening forces students to slow down and hear the substance of what's being said; when reading, it's easy to skim and miss key points. The key to making audio and video feedback a time-saving technique for a facilitator—rather than a time sink—is not to get too hung up on the quality of the audio or video. If you're producing audio or video to have students learn key pieces of content, aiming for a high-quality end product makes sense. But if you're simply trying to deliver feedback by putting voice to your ideas, then you don't need to do any editing or production. A simple screen recording or voice memo will truly suffice.

Learners, generally speaking, really appreciate having individualized feedback and will likely be grateful for any opportunity to see how a real person really understands their work and ideas. And it can be pleasurable as a facilitator to see immediately what the impact is of the learning material you've designed when you can take the time to appreciate and acknowledge learners' efforts in the course.

Takeaways

- **Students need to know how they're doing throughout the entire course, not just at the end.** You can't wait to let learners know if they are understanding the material or not. Build in opportunities for learners to self-correct, take more time, or get more information all throughout the learning experience.

- **Align the assessment type with your course goals.** When deciding how you best want to understand or gauge your student's learning, consider thinking first about the student and what feedback you think would be most helpful for them to receive in your course: Do they need right or wrong answers? Would they be better off self-reflecting? Try to align the approach of how they'll receive feedback with how easily they'll be able to understand their progress and learning in the course.

- **When possible, give students choices.** If there are multiple ways a learner can demonstrate that they've learned something, give them the choice! Learners will appreciate having the agency to decide how they best want to represent or demonstrate to you that they understand the course content.

- **Automated feedback can be great under the right circumstances.** A lot of learning designers overdo automated feedback because it saves them time. Consider the impact for your learners on receiving automated feedback. Will it impact their learning? Will it not have much impact? Try to make your choice in alignment with how your learners will experience getting feedback.

- **Less is more when it comes to individualized feedback.** If you are giving each student an individualized feedback response, remember that they can only process so much information. Highlight broad areas for improvement, not every area in need of change.

Reviewing Your Learning Experience

Think about what it's like to make a batch of pancakes on a griddle. You've got your batter mixed up and the griddle is hot. You take out your ladle, spoon out some batter, and pour it onto the griddle. Odds are that the first pancake is probably not perfect. Maybe it's a little undercooked in the middle, or your edges got a little lopsided. But by the time you make your second, then your third, you probably have a better feel for just how much batter to put on the pan and just how long to wait until the pancake is ready to flip over. Your pancakes improve every time you put a new one on the griddle.

Offering a new learning experience for the first time is a lot like making a first pancake. If you went through the entire design process and did all of the challenging work of considering who your learners are, how they'll experience the online learning interface, and what it will be like for them to build a community, the raw ingredients of your learning experience are probably pretty good. But there are probably some details that aren't going to be quite right or a few things that you could change to make the course better. Just as with making pancakes, every time you have the chance to run and offer a learning experience, you'll probably get even more skills, experience, and practice to improve it. It's rare that you'll need to go back and "redo" the entire course design from start to finish. But it's almost impossible to imagine a perfect first run at offering a course.

You need clear information and feedback to know what to improve, however. You might not know that your first pancake is undercooked until you take a bite of it yourself; the imperfections are not always obvious from the outside. Similarly, for a course, it won't always be clear to you, as the designer, what is not working. That's where you need feedback from within the course experience itself: from your learners, from data about your learners' performance, and from analytics gathered within the course experience's platform.

Reaching the end of a learning design experience feels like coming full circle. At the end of a course, learners go back to where they started. They can see whether they accomplished the outcomes of the course, and at the same time, assess whether they had the experience they had expected at the beginning. As the designer, you also return to where you started. You'll see whether the learners did, in fact, do what you had designed and to what extent your design supported— or limited—your learners' abilities to be successful.

For the learning designer, the end of the course often feels like yet another beginning. Hopefully, you have kept track of how your students were engaging with the experience throughout the course. By the time you get to the end, you have the unique opportunity to look at all the information that you've been gathering throughout the course and take the time to make sense of it all.

Looking back will better prepare you to look forward.

Learning from the Learners

Your most valuable source of information for improving the course will come from the learners, the users, and the course itself. A lot of learning designers and facilitators will distribute one survey at the end of the course and call it a day. While a survey is a great tool, it will only give you one window into what learners' impressions and experiences of the course were like. Even if you are operating without many resources or much time, try out a variety of approaches for getting feedback from your learners so that you can have the clearest possible picture of what the user experience of your course was like.

That said, don't overtax your learners' time and energy in completing additional work beyond their requirements for the course itself. Make choices about gathering feedback creatively and judiciously while exploring the full range of options available to you.

How to Ask Learners for Feedback

Consider all the options for receiving feedback that are at your disposal. You likely will not take advantage of all these options at once. Instead, pick the approach that best aligns with the information you need to improve your course for the future.

Feedback Surveys

A survey is probably the most common way that learning designers and facilitators receive feedback on their learners' course experiences. Surveys are easy to distribute, they're a low-touch intervention, and they can scale easily, regardless of the number of learners enrolled in your course. As shown in Chapter 2, "Learning About Your Learners," surveys are a great tool for learning some basics about who your learners are and for aggregating impressions at scale. When it comes to using a survey at the end of your course, a survey can provide an "at-a-glance" impression of learners' perceptions of your course's success.

End-of-course surveys should be very short and highly specific. You should ask no more than 10 multiple-choice or Likert scale questions (ranking on a scale from 1 to 10) in this type of survey. Consider creating space for one or two open-ended questions beyond the 10 multiple-choice or Likert scale questions, depending on what exactly you want to learn, but once you start to ask any more than 10 questions, you'll notice that survey participation will probably drop off. If you want to improve your chances of a high response rate, make it as easy for your learners to answer the questions as possible.

> **NOTE** LIKERT SCALE
>
> If you're unfamiliar with a Likert scale, it's any kind of question that asks a reader to rank an experience on a numerical scale, most commonly from 1 to 10, but occasionally the range will be smaller, such as from 1 to 5. An example Likert scale question could be:
>
> "On a scale of 1 to 10 with "1" representing a low score and "10" representing a high score, to what extent did you feel like you learned a new skill from taking this course?"

A survey is not a good place to ask, for example, about a learner's favorite activity or about how they would describe their favorite and least favorite parts of the course. A survey is a great place, on the other hand, to ask about their overall impressions of the experience and whether they felt like they achieved the outcomes of the course.

Some good examples of question types for an end-of-course learning experience survey could include:

1. By the end of the course, how much did your understanding of [insert content matter here] grow?

    a. It grew a lot.

    b. It grew a bit.

    c. It didn't grow at all.

2. How well-connected did you feel to the instructor in this course?

    a. Extremely well-connected

    b. Somewhat well-connected

    c. Barely connected

    d. Not at all connected

3. How well-connected did you feel to your peers in this course?

    a. Extremely well-connected

    b. Somewhat well-connected

    c. Barely connected

    d. Not at all connected

4. How was the pacing of the course?

    a. It went too fast.

    b. It went too slowly.

    c. It was just the right pace.

5. How manageable did the workload for this course feel?

    a. Extremely manageable

    b. Somewhat manageable

    c. Not at all manageable

End-of-course surveys are also very useful if you're in a position where you might need to justify the business value of the course and you need data to suggest that your course could easily acquire new users or customers. A lot of business end-user surveys include a Net Promoter Score (NPS) to determine the likelihood that the user or customer would recommend the service or experience to someone else. In the case of an end-of-course survey, you could use an NPS question to ask your learners whether they would promote your course to someone else in their personal network. An example NPS question for an end-of-course survey might be:

> On a scale of 1 to 10, how likely are you to recommend this course to a friend or colleague? (1 = would likely not recommend, 10 = would likely highly recommend)

Learning is social, so when learners can be advocates for your course and recommend it to others, you have demonstrable data to suggest that you've built a community of learners who would be willing to share the value of the learning experience they had.

Other survey question types will largely be dependent on context. We could have written (and many others have written!) entire books about effective survey design. If you know that you will need to write a survey to assess the efficacy of your course, we'd highly recommend consulting with resources that can offer you an even deeper dive into offering practical tips for writing good survey questions.

End-of-Course Learner Reflections

If you have the room or time in your course design, create a small assignment for learners to complete where you ask them to reflect on their experience in the course. To incentivize completing this reflection, consider offering an additional credit or "make-up" points for completing the reflection. That said, this external motivation may not be necessary; many learners may be intrinsically motivated to submit a reflection to share their experiences. Before asking learners to reflect on their experience and submit open-ended feedback, you might even offer a bit of context for why you're requesting their written feedback beyond a survey. You could share with your learners the following language either in writing, as in a course announcement or email, or even in a short video from your voice and perspective:

> Just like you, I'm learning all of the time and strive to improve in the work that I do. The best way for me to create better course experiences for others in the future is by hearing about your experience as a learner and what it meant for you to be in this class over the course of this particular term.

> In this reflection assignment, I encourage you to take as much or as little time as you'd like to share what you found most rewarding, most disappointing, and most challenging about the course. You might speak to the learning tools we used in this course, as well as the materials, activities, and assignments we engaged in. You can engage with all of or none of these things when you write your response. You can write one sentence, or you can write a paragraph. Everything you share is helpful. Keep in mind that I read your responses carefully before planning the course for the next time I offer it. Thank you for taking the time to share your experiences! They really do make a difference.

Offering this kind of open-ended prompt with a few guided responses can help learners make sense of their experience while also giving you valuable information about whatever sticks out to them in a more qualitative way than in a survey. You will likely receive fewer responses on open-ended reflections than you will on close-ended surveys, but there are valuable things you can glean when you invite learners to share what they experienced in their own words.

Post-Course Interviews

It can be very useful to talk to learners one-on-one about what they most liked or found most challenging about your course. Post-course interviews can be challenging and time-consuming both to coordinate and facilitate, however. If you know you want to have some one-on-one conversations with your learners about their experiences of taking the course, you will likely have the most success if you schedule your interviews during the final week of the course itself. With a small group, you might schedule the equivalent of 15-minute "exit interviews" with a clear set of just one to two questions to ask each student. Some examples of "exit interview"-style questions might include:

- Tell me about the one most meaningful experience you had in this course.
- Tell me about the one biggest frustration you experienced in this course.

Asking learners to tell you a story about what came up for them, rather than asking a leading question or asking students to rate their experiences out loud, will help you make the most of having a real-time conversation.

How to Get Feedback Without Asking for It

Getting direct feedback from your learners is ideal, but, inevitably, you won't get to hear from everyone. Unfortunately, that means there will be valuable perspectives you'll miss from those who do not have the time, capacity, or interest in giving you direct feedback on their learning experience.

Don't get stuck relying upon the feedback you solicit directly. Consider what you can observe in the course itself and how the learner experiences within the online course can give you a sense of what's working (or not) for everyone.

Analyzing Course Click Data

Whether you are using a learning management system (LMS) or offering your course through a website, you'll have click-rate data you can analyze. Most modern LMS platforms and websites offer robust analytics dashboards that will enable you to see how often particular resources, assignments, and links within the course were clicked. Looking at this data will give you a clearer sense of which resources learners returned to repeatedly and which they didn't think were as meaningful.

Click data from course resources could help you determine:

- Popularity of particular resources
- Usefulness of particular resources
- Timeliness of particular resources

Extrapolating this information could then help:

- Redesign resources in the course to resemble the popular ones.
- Omit unpopular resources or add in new resources that support the popular ones.

Looking at click rates likely will not tell you why certain resources were perceived as more valuable than others. Simply put, you won't get the full picture. But this data may give you enough information to prioritize what learners were accessing throughout the course. That will help streamline the course and help your learners see the best and clearest content.

Analyzing Course and Assignment Completion Data

Seeing patterns in how, when, and where learners successfully completed course content can give you a lot of information about how well the course was paced, what kinds of assignments were the most engaging, and how balanced the workload may have felt for learners. You might notice particular trends specifically for the following areas:

- **Assignment Engagement:** Notice if any assignments were completed more often by a majority of learners than others. If there are assignments that were rarely turned in completed, consider the implications: Was that assignment too challenging? Were you asking for too much? Or was the assignment sequenced at the wrong time?

- **Attrition:** Look at how many learners began the course, but then quit or dropped out before it ended. Then look at the timing. When in the course sequence did learners decide to drop the course? Naturally, you'll likely see patterns in drop rates at the beginning of the course since some learners may recognize that the pacing and organization of the course is not what they expected. Beyond those common patterns, you'll want to examine where you see other time periods for frequent drops, if any. That data can tell you a lot about the workload, pacing, and difficulty of content at different points in the course experience.

- **Time to Completion:** Many modern learning management systems or websites will include time spent in browser or in tab on a particular task. A word of caution that this metric may be misleading; different people process information at different paces, which is expected and understandable. But you may still want to look at overall patterns and trends, especially if you're noticing that there's a pattern in how users are spending a particularly long (or short) time on particular tasks. Look at the aggregate rather than the individual in this case; the averages will give you more information than any one individual data point will. That aggregated information should help you determine whether activities and assignments are sequenced and planned effectively.

Making Sense of Your Review

After gathering a mountain of evidence about the learning experience, it's easy to feel overwhelmed. You'll likely see patterns emerge as you review the data that you've gathered. The key is to process and communicate those patterns both for yourself and for any stakeholders invested in understanding the learning experience you've designed. There is no better time than immediately after the learning experience has concluded to assess how your learning experience went. Your reflections will be fresher that way. To that end, we encourage you to make sense of your learner feedback and your own experiences observing or facilitating the course within one to two weeks after the learning experience has finished.

WRITING A REFLECTION

If you've got limited time to review the feedback about your course, writing a short individual reflection will help you process and make sense of the information you encountered when gathering your feedback. Here are questions you could answer in bullet points for yourself:

- What's my gut reaction to how the course went? Did it seem like students had a good, bad, or just an OK experience?
- How am I feeling now that the course is over?
- What data point stood out the most?
- What data point surprised me the most?
- What's the biggest strength that I saw in the course based on the data I gathered?
- What's the biggest weakness or area of concern that I saw in the course based on the data I gathered?
- What's just one thing I could do differently with the course the next time I design or offer it?

Answering these questions could take you anywhere from 30–60 minutes, depending on how much detail you want to use in responding to them. But answering these kinds of questions should start to focus your analysis and understanding of the course and give you a much stronger start when and if you have the opportunity to offer the learning experience again.

With More Time: Creating a Review Memo

You should start with the "quick start" reflection questions before you try to write about your learning experience for anyone else. Designing and facilitating a course can be an intense and deeply personal experience, so give yourself the space to process those feelings and jot down your observations privately before you attempt to make even greater sense of them.

Use the notes from your individual reflection to inform the writing of a review memo where you bring together what you noticed and experienced in alignment with the data you gathered and in the context of the course's original goals and outcomes. There may be a lot of information that you gather in your review that's not that useful. For example, the survey results you gather may not point you to very many clear conclusions about the course. That's where your memo comes in: You can separate the extraneous or unhelpful findings from the ideas that you actually act upon.

Consider structuring your memo with the following template:

ONE-PAGE REVIEW MEMO TEMPLATE

Section 1: Course Goals and Outcomes

Section 2: Summary of Learner Feedback

Prioritize including any data you have about learners' satisfaction and learners' perceptions of their abilities to achieve the course outcomes. Focus on aggregated data, but highlight one to two qualitative comments from learners, taken from either their reflections, focus group questions, or any open-ended survey questions.

Section 3: Summary of Course Data

Prioritize including any data you have about learner completion rates and most popular/most accessed resources in your course.

Section 4: Analysis

Summarize your top 2-3 conclusions that you reached based on reviewing the learner feedback and the course data. These top 2-3 conclusions should highlight both things that worked in the course and things that didn't work. Try identifying one quality of the course that worked well and one quality of the course that didn't work as well.

Section 5: Areas for Growth and Redevelopment

Identify 2-3 parts of the course that are in need of revision based on the feedback and analysis you've conducted. If your document is getting long, this section could be combined with Section 4.

The purpose of your memo should be to help you and any stakeholders in your course prioritize any revisions that may need to be made when offering the learning experience again in the future.

Preparing Your Course for Someone Else

Saying "goodbye" when a course is over can feel bittersweet, especially if you spent a lot of hours designing, conceptualizing, and reconceptualizing the course over multiple iterations. It's possible that you'll get to redesign and facilitate your own course again, but a lot of learning designers find themselves in situations where they're asked to pass along and share their course materials with someone else. Another designer may be tasked to redesign the course you've built, or another facilitator may use portions of or the entirety of your course for their own learning experience.

If you find yourself in that situation, there are a few steps you can take immediately after you've finished offering the course to make it easier for someone else to orient effectively to the course materials and start off in the right direction.

Consider creating a short "instructor's guide" to give someone who may be redesigning or facilitating the learning experience an inside understanding of what they need to know about the course before it launches again. In this guide, include the following information:

- An overview of the course's purpose
- A brief description of the primary audience(s) for the course
- A simplified learning map to give an understanding of the course's direction and pacing (consider sharing the learning map you developed per the advice in Chapter 3, "Setting the Foundation")
- A bullet-point list of the biggest challenges you noticed when designing and facilitating the course
- A bullet-point list of tips you'd offer to yourself if you could teach the course for the first time again

If you don't have the time, energy, or resources to create such a guide, you could also jot down a few quick thoughts in response to one or both of the following prompts:

- What are one or two things that you think someone who is not you may need to know about the design and implementation of this course?
- If you could talk to yourself about the course and offer advice, what would you say?

Importantly, if you're preparing someone else to engage with your course, remember that getting them excited about the course is equally as important as preparing them to facilitate the material well. Consider including a couple of quotes that you may have encountered in the learner surveys or reflections about what learners enjoyed in the course. Just as positive emotions are a powerful motivator for learners, so too will positive emotions motivate and inspire any future designers and facilitators.

Celebrating Your Success

You've accomplished something remarkable by designing an effective online learning experience. Recognize the work you've done in understanding who your learners are and what the possibilities are for engaging with them online. As you reflect on how your learning experience went, take the time to be present in your accomplishments and feel proud of the work that you did. Celebrating your success will help you not only feel refreshed when it comes to making any revisions, but it will also allow you to remain energized, hopeful, and excited about designing new learning experiences in the future.

Being an effective learning designer requires being flexible and responsive to an ever-changing environment. You have a unique set of skills as a learning designer. You have to create an experience that is structured and easy for users to understand, while also being responsive to different learners' needs and interests as you encounter them. That's not an easy balance to strike, and you can't expect to get it right 100 percent of the time. Staying compassionate, open, and eager to learn will go a long way toward reaching that balance and designing meaningful learning experiences for everyone.

Takeaways

- **Don't expect a class to run perfectly.** There will always be room for growth and improvement.
- **Get feedback directly from learners if you can.** Hearing what their experiences were like with the course can guide your revisions for future offerings.
- **Look to course analytics, like click-rate data and downloads, to get a feel for popular or valuable materials.** The metrics won't tell the whole story, but they are an important data point for recognizing and appreciating what learners found valuable.
- **Reflect on what you learned.** Don't wait too long to sum up your own takeaways and experiences. Write a brief reflection on what worked and what didn't. Your fresh knowledge will be the most valuable.
- **Celebrate!** Designing a course is no small feat. Revel in your accomplishment!

INDEX

ACKNOWLEDGMENTS

Good writing happens in community, and we are tremendously grateful for the community of writers who have supported our work on this book. We'd first like to thank the wonderfully supportive team at Rosenfeld Media who made this book a reality. Lou, thank you for believing in our vision for this book and coaching us through how to make the ideas here practical, useful, and engaging for readers. Marta, we are so grateful for your guidance, coaching, support, and critically important feedback all along the way. This would not be the book it is today without you. You helped clarify our ideas, punch up our prose, and get right to the point. We had several expert peer reviewers provide extensive feedback that helped shape and improve this book. Leilani Serafin, Daniel Stanford, and Niya Bond, your notes and close reading made this book more applicable, helpful, and interesting. We are so grateful for your time, energy, and support!

Several learning designers across the country spoke with us about their experiences and examples of effective learning design. Only a small portion could go into this book, but we want to acknowledge all of those who took time out of their day to engage with us: Max Riggsbee, Santanu Vasant, Tiffany Brown, Callista Dawson, Andreina Parisi-Amon, Christina Long, Anne Fensie, Devin Chaloux, Katherine Fisne, and Renata Mares. Thank you!

Thank you to our friends and colleagues from the Online Writing Instruction community whose ideas also informed the writing of this book, particularly Heidi Skurat Harris and Mary Stewart.

Finally, we could not possibly have completed this book without the support of our partners, Kevin Schenthal and Brenda Hadenfeldt. They tolerated our time writing in the evenings, weekends, and the little hours in between. Thank you for supporting us and everything that it took to write this!

 **Rosenfeld**®

Dear Reader,

Thanks very much for purchasing this book. There's a story behind it and every product we create at Rosenfeld Media.

Since the early 1990s, I've been a User Experience consultant, conference presenter, workshop instructor, and author. (I'm probably best-known for having cowritten *Information Architecture for the Web and Beyond*.) In each of these roles, I've been frustrated by the missed opportunities to apply UX principles and practices.

I started Rosenfeld Media in 2005 with the goal of publishing books whose design and development showed that a publisher could practice what it preached. Since then, we've expanded into producing industry-leading conferences and workshops. In all cases, UX has helped us create better, more successful products—just as you would expect. From employing user research to drive the design of our books and conference programs, to working closely with our conference speakers on their talks, to caring deeply about customer service, we practice what we preach every day.

Please visit rosenfeldmedia.com to learn more about our **conferences, workshops, free communities,** and **other great resources** that we've made for you. And send your ideas, suggestions, and concerns my way: louis@rosenfeldmedia.com

I'd love to hear from you, and I hope you enjoy the book!

Lou Rosenfeld,
Publisher

RECENT TITLES FROM ROSENFELD MEDIA

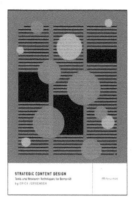

Get a great discount on a Rosenfeld Media book:
visit rfld.me/deal to learn more.

SELECTED TITLES FROM ROSENFELD MEDIA

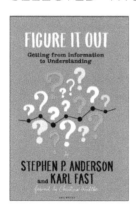

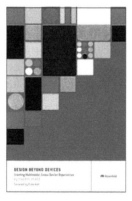

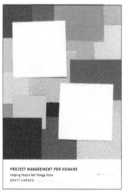

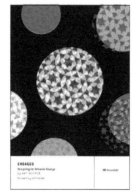

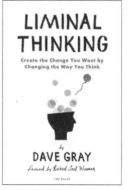

View our full catalog at rosenfeldmedia.com/books

ABOUT THE AUTHORS

Dr. Jenae Cohn writes and speaks about online teaching and learning for international audiences. She currently works as the Executive Director of the Center for Teaching and Learning at University of California, Berkeley, and has held prior roles at California State University, Sacramento, Stanford University, and University of California, Davis. She has designed resources for teachers, facilitators, and coaches on ways to improve learner engagement online and is a frequent contributor to *The Chronicle of Higher Education, Faculty Focus,* and other trade publications dedicated to teaching and learning. She is the author of the book, *Skim, Dive, Surface: Teaching Digital Reading* (West Virginia University Press, 2021). Learn more about Jenae at jenaecohn.net, on Twitter, or LinkedIn.

Michael Greer is an independent writer and editor based in Boulder, Colorado. Michael has taught online courses in writing, editing, and multimedia and served as founding editor of the journal *Research in Online Literacy Education.* Michael is co-author of the celebrated *The Little, Brown Handbook* and co-author of the forthcoming *Multimedia with a Purpose* (Stylus Press). He writes about user-centered design, interactive media, and digital publishing.

CPSIA information can be obtained
at www.ICGtesting.com
Printed in the USA
JSHW041653160623
43083JS00003BA/1